It took The Amazing Kreskin over twenty years to perfect his mind-boggling feats. Now he shows you how to duplicate his best!

How would you like to . . .

★ Render a pal unable to get up off the floor?
★ Levitate a table in a scary séance?
★ Create an imaginary insect for your bratty sister to swat away?
★ Make Kreskin-like predictions in front of baffled friends?
★ Prevent a person from rising from a chair through "hypnosis"?
★ Perform never-before-seen stunts with a simple deck of cards?

If you answered "yes" to any of the above, this amazing book of stunts is for you!

HOW TO BE
A FAKE
KRESKIN

THE AMAZING KRESKIN

PHOTOGRAPHS BY DAVID ODETTE

St. Martin's Paperbacks

HOW TO BE A FAKE KRESKIN

Copyright © 1996 by Kreskin.

Photographs throughout text by David Odette.

ISBN: 0-312-95871-4

Printed in the United States of America

St. Martin's Paperbacks trade paperback edition/October 1996

10 9 8 7 6 5 4 3 2 1

TO MOM AND TO JENNIE CHUBB...
THE TWO WOMEN WHO HAVE GIVEN ME
SPIRITUAL SUPPORT THROUGHOUT MY LIFE.

From the first day I began writing this book I had planned, as part of my dedication, a tribute to my dear friend Robert Lund of Marshall, Michigan, a brilliant newspaperman. In his retirement he amassed a monumental museum of information and memorabilia about the mystery workers in the entertainment field through our history. He was an inspiring supporter of my work and was immensely enthusiastic about this book and the very nature of its contents. I can hear him even today saying to me: "Kreskin, this is the best answer to your critics and skeptics that you could possibly produce." While he is no longer with us, I feel his presence in every page of this book.

ACKNOWLEDGMENTS

It would have been more than "amazing" to have brought this to fruition without editorial and advisory support fron Richard Hatch, David Meyers, and Bob Lund.

CONTENTS

PREFACE

BY DAVID MEYER

I have a friend who phones me every year before he leaves to spend two weeks in Saudi Arabia. He is not an oil man, a salesman, an importer or a government official. Neither is he going there on vacation. He just keeps getting invited back.

He is a man who often cannot keep track of the key to the hotel room where he is staying—and by now he should be able to, as he spends over three hundred days of the year "on the road" or "in the air" and (as you may have already guessed) "on stage." And yet he can find, without the assistance of anyone in the audience or backstage, without the use of electronic devices or any concealed help of any kind, his paycheck, which is hidden during the course of his performance. (If he doesn't find that check, wherever it may be in the theater, he doesn't get paid, and he is very well paid.)

He is also the man who set out to find, hidden somewhere in the vastness of New York City, Robin Leach, the well-known host of the television program "Lifestyles of the Rich and Famous." My friend, racing against the clock and under the eyes of countless spectators, was successful in his hunt for Mr. Leach. I am quick to add that, when hidden, Mr. Leach neither helped get himself found nor thought he *would* be found. The thousands who watched this experiment probably had the same idea, but they soon learned just how good my friend is at what he does.

Another fact from having known him for over ten years: He reads a book in twenty minutes or less and five years later remembers its contents. There are books which have particularly impressed him from which he can quote ten years later. And if he likes a book enough, he reads it again, then again. While I can't pretend to know all the subjects that interest him, in our many conversations I have learned a great deal from him about psychology, hypnotism, psychic research, stage illusions, Dracula, show business and numerous other subjects— some of which, I'm sorry to admit, *I* can't remember!

The favorite works of his youth? One of these was "Mandrake the Magician," the comic strip character created by Lee Falk and Phil Davis. My friend, who taught himself to read at the age of five, was fascinated by the fictitious Mandrake, a hero who accomplished feats purely by mental influence, unaided by sleight of hand deception or the trickery of a stage magician. As a youth he sought to emulate the marvelous Mandrake. Today he embodies what Mandrake was all about, for he creates a performance purely through the guided interplay of the audience's imagination with the performer's suggestions and sensitivity. At a recent meeting with Mandrake's creator, Lee Falk told my friend that he had come as close as humanly possible to the ideal espoused by this famous fictional character.

If I could choose one word to describe this man, *boundless* might be the adjective to use. He has boundless energy and enthusiasm. When he begins a performance (whether it be in a nightclub, a college or corporate auditorium, or before a vast crowd at a state fair) he rushes on stage: a tall, thin, bespectacled bundle of energy, grinning from ear to ear and seeming to give those before him a mental "group hug" to which everyone instinctively responds. Here is a man who loves life, loves his audience and loves what he does!

Now all the standard rules of showmanship insist that a performer immediately begin with one of his strongest effects: a singer sings a familiar hit, a comedian tells one of his funniest jokes. But my friend's performance is anything but standard. He begins by letting his audience get to know him. He may recount an incident from one of his record eighty-eight appearances on the "Tonight Show" or tell about the show business legend that Johnny Carson was inspired to create—the clumsy yet sage "Carnac the Magnificent" character—after seeing my friend trip and fall on his first (of many!) appearances on "The Steve Allen Show." David Letterman, Larry King, Regis and Kathie Lee and a host of other hosts have invited him to appear on their shows as well. I particularly enjoy his appearances with Letterman, that raconteur of ridicule, who always treats my friend, not with the usual verbal jabs or sarcasm, but with great kindness and affection. Even when Mr. Letterman interrupts my friend a few dozen times during the performance of an impromptu mental feat, it is all a part of the fun. The rapport between the two is very apparent and real.

Audiences, too, find it easy to share his delight when he describes some episode in his varied show business career. Although it might come as a surprise to many, he is an accomplished pianist. So good, in fact, he has played Carnegie Hall—the dream of untold performers! He has appeared in performance with symphony orchestras across the country and in Canada. This is not the usual "sideline" of so many other performers. I still recall visiting him in his hotel suite in Chicago several years ago and hearing him play beautifully for his own enjoyment and mine—and no telling how many other guests who might have heard him through the walls and hall!

He often begins his performance proper with a feat of magic. Perhaps he'll borrow a finger ring from two persons in the audience. In an instant and in clear view he will link these borrowed rings together. Or he might produce an ice-cold glass of water from an empty bag while both his wrists are held securely by audience volunteers. He is an acknowledged master of the magical arts; though, like his piano playing, he regards this skill merely as an avocation. It is his on- and off-stage explorations of the mysteries of the mind that are his true vocation.

After he has let the audience know a little about himself, it is his turn to get to know his audience. He does this in a sophisticated display of nonverbal communication. Sitting alone onstage, doodling aimlessly on a writing pad to clear his mind, he picks up, by thought alone, odd bits of information from throughout the auditorium. Someone's phone number rings a bell. A mother's maiden name comes through to him. A birth date. An anniversary. No one is more astonished than those persons in the audience concentrating on these things, unless it is my friend himself, who still gets caught off guard by the stray thoughts he picks up. Often he will turn the experiment around, concentrating on a number or a picture and attempting to project it to the audience. There is always a gasp of recognition from those who succeed in tuning in to his thoughts. "You see how easy it is!" He chuckles. "Any twelve-year-old can do what I do . . . with forty years' practice."

He brings the first half of his performance to a dramatic close with his signature piece: the search for his hidden paycheck. The details of this feat are discussed later in this book, but I should mention that the longer it takes my friend to find his check, the more perversely interested his audience seems to become. I can only imagine what memories of previous performances must come to mind each time he undertakes this perilous feat. "Where will the committee from the audience have hidden my check this time? Never again in a baby's diaper! Nor beneath the old gentleman's dental plate! Or in a light suspended from the ceiling of the theater!"

The second half of my friend's performance explores the mind's responses to heighten suggestibility. Inviting as many as fifty audience members to join him onstage, he soon has them seeing things that do *not* exist, such as flying birds, UFOs or family pets, and not seeing things that do exist, such as the dean of a university or the mayor of a city who are somehow overlooked or not even perceived as standing on the stage. One person perspires in the imagined heat of the desert; another shivers against an arctic wind. One may find it impossible to remember his name, another may find she cannot count past seven or for some reason seems to have eleven fingers. All this occurs, my friend will insist, without benefit of any so-called hypnotic trance. His finale is a re-creation of a classic "post-suggestion test." As the volunteers are thanked and dismissed they begin to walk off stage. But wait! This person stops and does a dance. That person begins to shake hands with half the members of the auditorium. Another removes his coat to put out an imaginary fire on a chair. The rest of the group may suddenly begin to sing "Happy Birthday." His audience loves it.

What is it about the way our minds work that allows us to be deceived? My friend's tenacious thirst for knowledge led him, at age eleven, to be granted access to the entire psychology section of the local public library. He experimented with hypnosis and the subtle techniques of nonverbal communication, playing a mental game of hide-and-seek with family and friends. He began to perform professionally as "The World's Youngest Hypnotist." Engagements continued through college as he completed work on a bachelor's degree in psychology at Seton Hall University. That institution has since granted him an honorary doctor of letters degree.

As his fascination with the mysteries of the mind grew, his reliance on the traditional techniques of both conjuring and hypnosis weakened to the point where he called both into question. Could his audiences be entertained without being deceived? Could they respond to suggestion without being hypnotized? Using his many performances as a living laboratory, he discovered that the answer to both questions was a resounding yes. In fact, he ultimately concluded that hypnosis was not only unnecessary but nonexistent! The so-called trance state of traditional hypnotists was simply a by-product of preconceived expectations and explicit suggestions much like the fairy-tale emperor's "new clothes." Once convinced of the truth of this discovery, he proclaimed it to the world, offering the first of his monetary challenges (originally ten thousand dollars, now one hundred thousand dollars) to anyone who can scientifically establish the existence of an independent and special hypnotic state.

My friend, who is traveling and performing nearly every day of the year, is known as the world's foremost mentalist. More importantly, he is a world-class entertainer. (Why else would they want him to return to Saudi Arabia every December, but to perform, astound and entertain?) He is a man who lives not only by his wits, talent, personality and charisma; he also lives by taking risks. He is The Amazing Kreskin.

The experiments you will read in this book are the easy explanations of feats he has performed, but they are *not* what takes place when Kreskin actually performs. No, these are the methods proposed by Kreskin's imitators and detractors. With this book, Kreskin has decided to expose those who believe they are exposing him. If the methods contained in this book were actually used by Kreskin, he would not be revealing them in this or any other book.

Whatever he does, Kreskin does wholeheartedly, with boundless energy and unbridled enthusiasm. His unabashed love of his work and of his audiences may recall to some the admitted influence of pioneering broadcaster Arthur Godfrey. And if he sometimes displays the fervor of a charismatic televangelist, he would admit the charge, having been an admirer of the communication skills of Bishop Sheen. Indeed, Kreskin is a missionary of the mind, winning converts to his enthusiasms with each performance. If the secret of Kreskin's phenomenal success had to be summed up in a single word, that word would be *sincerity*.

"And if you can fake that," says Kreskin, "you won't need the rest of this book."

I am not surprised Kreskin has published *How to Be a Fake Kreskin*. Knowing him as long as I have, anything he might do—whether to entertain or to seek out truths—would not surprise me.

David Meyer
Publisher and Historian

INTRODUCTION

Recently writers posing as "experts" have been advertising high-priced books and manuscripts purporting, among other things, to explain the methods I use in my worldwide concert performances. Having a keen interest in this topic, I naturally lost little time securing copies of these materials. Unfortunately, in today's society, anyone posing as a journalist is given free rein to publish anything about anyone, with little regard for the truth. Rather than sacrifice time and money pursuing legal action to protect other potential consumers from these rip-off artists, I have decided to "expose the exposers," offering in book form not only their "secrets," but numerous more practical "solutions" of my own.

For more than forty years I have collected various "explanations" of my work and shared these ideas with my audiences. The contrast between these "theories" and what my audiences actually experience always makes these discussions one of the humorous highlights of my concerts. With apologies to David Letterman, here is my own "Top Ten List" of "how I do what I do."

KRESKIN'S TOP TEN LIST

10. Kreskin's mother spies on the audience with binoculars from the rafters and transmits the information to him on a miniature radio receiver hidden in his eyeglass frames.

9. Kreskin achieves X-ray vision by shining a special intense light on the audience to render packages and envelopes transparent.

8. Kreskin hires a private eye to dig up dirt on his audience before each show.

7. The pads and pencils Kreskin gives the audience to use have radar systems imbedded in them.

6. Kreskin forces audience members to write their innermost thoughts on a special pad with carbon paper hidden inside.

5. Kreskin can make anyone say anything anytime through the power of suggestion.

4. Kreskin steals information when no one is looking.

3. It's all done with stooges.

2. Kreskin is just a darn good guesser.

1. Kreskin is the luckiest man alive.

If you have ever wanted to imitate some of my feats, I encourage you to try some of the stunts I teach here. And even if you have only an armchair interest in such things, I sincerely hope that this modest volume will save you money you might otherwise have spent on the poorly produced and overpriced crackpot exposés.

ESPecially,
KRESKIN

HOW TO BE
A FAKE
KRESKIN

1
TAKE MY SUGGESTION...PLEASE!

Of the many theories put forth over the years to explain my work, probably the most common has been that my performances are pre-arranged and that the volunteer subjects are actually paid assistants (*"stooges"* in the language of show business) trained to act out my demonstrations. Perhaps this would make sense were it possible to explain why, after I have spent so many years in the public limelight, not one of these "subjects" has come forward to expose me. Given the enormous sums the tabloid press would be willing to pay for such a fantastic story, any one of literally thousands of subjects would long ago have either publicly cashed in on the conspiracy or privately blackmailed me into bankruptcy were such an outrageous charge even remotely true.

To suggest that the basis for my demonstrations is trickery begs the question and ignores the fact that I have never claimed any supernatural powers or special psychic abilities. As a showman, I naturally reserve the right to embellish my performances with magical touches that

heighten the dramatic value of my work without dimin-
ishing its legitimacy. I am, after all, an entertainer, not a
guinea pig!

It might well surprise my critics to learn that I actually
sympathize with their skepticism. When you have made
a career of demonstrating unusual abilities, you tend to
view similar claims by others with a skeptic's eye, knowing firsthand how difficult it is to achieve such things
legitimately. As a case in point, after more than forty
years both researching and demonstrating the power of
suggestion, I have become absolutely convinced that the
so-called state of hypnosis simply does not exist. In other
words, there is no special state of mind, condition or
trance that can be uniquely characterized as hypnotic.
This bold statement has often been misunderstood. Some
say I am claiming that hypnosis is a trick—totally fake.
Others argue that I am merely playing with semantics,
substituting one definition for another. And there are still
others who say that my claim is simply a clever way to
avoid the legal ramifications associated with a demonstration of hypnosis.

The latter statement is especially ignorant. As I have
demonstrated publicly for years, any phenomena that
can be produced through suggestion with someone apparently in the hypnotic state can just as readily be produced without a hypnotic state, simply by properly
combining persuasion and suggestion with an active and
attentive imagination. When a hypnotist suggests to subjects on a stage that they are getting cold and they actually become chilled, this is not a trick, but neither is it
more mysterious a phenomenon than when we watch a
Hitchcock movie and become so frightened that we get

goose bumps. This "chiller" has induced a physiological reaction, raising the surface of our flesh without altering the temperature of our environment. Years ago, on a PBS science report, I claimed that viewers nationwide would swallow uncontrollably at my suggestion. The report has been rebroadcast so many times that you may recall seeing me take a lemon and graphically describe its sour taste. I then carefully cut the lemon open and—on camera—deliberately sucked on it. On our first taping we had to stop and start over again because the camera crew was salivating so profusely that their swallowing caused them to miss their cues! All across the country, thousands, young and old alike, wrote in to report the success of this national experiment. Was it magic or trickery, fake? Of course not! Neither did it require a hypnotic trance.

People often ask, when seeing a demonstration of "hypnosis," what the subjects are "under." The pseudoscientific responses such as "semiconscious state," "trancelike state," "superconscious state" and so on are meaningless double-talk. The subjects are not "under" anything, since every test known to science clearly demonstrates they are totally conscious and wide-awake. They are simply responding to my suggestions or those of the "hypnotist." This is not just playacting, although often someone who *is* playacting may suddenly become uncritical in his or her thinking and begin to respond as though "hypnotized." Such a person is simply becoming open to suggestion and responding to the stimulation of an active imagination.

If you see such a demonstration in public, it will fall into one of five categories. In the first, the so-called hypnotist works with a group of onstage assistants who are, in fact, plants or stooges, referred to in the fake hypnotic racket as *"horses,"* paid actors who travel with the hypnotist and are simply faking their responses. Frankly, such a performance is rarely seen today, although it was quite common in the heyday of vaudeville. Second, the subjects are legitimate and the hypnotist thinks he is hypnotizing them, but some of them have been trained to respond quickly to his suggestions, being, in fact, preconditioned assistants rather than spontaneous volunteers from the audience. This is a fairly common practice and often these suggestible subjects are paid to travel with the hypnotist's show, much like the "horses" of an earlier era. Third, the hypnotist actually works with total strangers, but whispers instructions to them, cueing them secretly to play along and fake their responses. This is often used by hypnotists who must do a very quick act and, in fact, in France, it is the most common form of stage hypnotism. Of course, return engagements are rare for such performers when they work for an organization or company, as the newly recruited stooges inevitably spread the word once the show is over. In the fourth case, the subjects are legitimate, bona fide, untrained volunteers from the audience and the hypnotist leads them through the standard techniques of inducing drowsiness, sleep, etc. He then has the subject recreate all the classic stunts of traditional clinical, experimental and theatrical hypnosis, causing the subjects to imagine they are famous people, or play with imaginary animals, experience biting cold, then tropical heat, etc. The fifth category is my way of presenting it: a pure demonstration of heightened suggestibility in which legitimate audience volunteers are not subjected to the mumbo-jumbo of hypnotic induc-

tion, but nonetheless rapidly behave as though hypnotized in response to persuasion, suggestion and an
activated imagination. There is, in fact, a sixth category
of demonstration, which takes things one step beyond
what was previously thought possible. This represents the
culmination of a dream of mine ever since, as a boy, I
was inspired by the comic strip exploits of Mandrake the
Magician. Created by Lee Falk, Mandrake was not merely
a sleight of hand artist, although he would occasionally
be seen in the strip giving public performances as an entertainer. But he was primarily a crime fighter, using his
unusual and mysterious hypnotic abilities to investigate
and vanquish criminals. He had the ability to "cloud
men's minds," compelling them to see things that did not
exist and respond irresistibly to his mental suggestions.
In my performances today, I regularly demonstrate my
own ability to influence total strangers onstage, causing
them to respond to suggestions without even telling them
verbally what the suggestions are!

Unfortunately, it is impossible for me to teach this ability—which has taken me years to perfect—within the
constraints of a book such as this. And, in fact, even if I
could communicate this knowledge effectively, there are
obvious ethical and legal considerations that would inhibit my doing so. But I can explain part of my success
with this demonstration and how I can consistently
achieve positive results so quickly, without resorting to
preconditioned volunteers or paid assistants. It is due in
part to what some psychologists have termed the *"faith-
prestige"* relationship that I have developed and maintain
with my audiences. After so many years before the public, both on stage and on television, most of those at-

tending my concerts are already quite familiar with my work and abilities. Their preexisting belief in those abilities actually helps me to demonstrate them. This is similar to the phenomenon that provides my friend David Letterman with a huge response to a joke that might only rate a chuckle if told by a talented but unknown comic. Knowing how truly funny Dave is makes him even funnier, just as peoples' confidence in my abilities confers on me the confidence to demonstrate them. The next time you have a chance to attend one of my performances, come up on stage when I reach the portion of the program where audience members are invited to volunteer. If you follow my instructions attentively, use your imagination actively and trust me completely, you will find that—perhaps thirty seconds after volunteering—when I challenge you to get out of your chair, you won't be able to do so. Or when I ask you to tell me your address, you not only can't tell me, but may actually not remember it for the next ten or fifteen minutes of the program!

Now let me show you how to fake a hypnotic demonstration.

KRESKIN'S ARM LEVITATION STUNT

One of the most famous clinical hypnotists was a psychiatrist, Dr. Milton H. Erickson. Erickson was quite theatrical in his own way, and although he limited his performances and entertainment to educational demonstrations for medical gatherings, he was not beneath resorting to the strategies and tricks of certain stage hypnotists. Often he would spend two or three hours

with subjects the night before a demonstration, precon-
ditioning the desired responses, so that when they answered his request for audience volunteers the next day,
they would respond rapidly to his suggestions, although
perceived by the rest of the gathering as new subjects.
My close friend, Dr. Maurice Bryant, an authority on
medical hypnosis, learned of this firsthand when he
worked with Erickson at a medical seminar.

Erickson made famous a hypnotic induction technique
in which the subject, seated in a chair, looks at his or her
hands, one of which then rises uncontrollably and involuntarily off the lap almost to the point of touching the
subject's face. This was dubbed the "arm levitation" and
was, in fact, developed by a Dr. Wolberg many years prior
to Erickson, although the latter rarely gave Wolberg any
credit. Actually, the community of medical hypnotists
share a worldview so myopic that they have *never* cred-
ited the true originators of this stunt, the nineteenth-
century stage hypnotists and mesmerists. I have in my
collection numerous photographs of turn-of-the century
hypnotists onstage, performing at a time when speed and
fast pacing were not required, causing their subjects' arms
to rise off a table and into the air as the subjects become
more susceptible to hypnosis. To teach this stunt would
not only take a considerable amount of time, but may, in
fact, not be a natural skill that anyone can acquire, as it
does demand a high degree of intuition. Basically, the
subject is talked to in such a way that when he or she
reacts, whether it is the right or left hand that starts to
move, the clinical hypnotist deceptively interprets the response as though it were precisely the one intended. This
is really an illusion based on equivocal interpretation. In

many respects, the arm levitation technique is a form of highly sophisticated conjuring, although the average medical practitioner would not only deny this, but most likely does not even comprehend the true dynamics involved. It is a wise hypnotist who knows who is hypnotizing whom—and in this case, it is really the hypnotist himself who is being hypnotized into believing he is producing a trance.

With this background, you are ready to learn and demonstrate the Kreskin arm levitation stunt. Let's assume you have chosen as your subject a young woman named Susan. Have her stand in a doorway facing your group, both her arms hanging at her sides. Now tell her to place her arms against the sides of the door frame, pressing her arms outward, away from her body, as hard as possible, and to continue pressing firmly for thirty to forty-five seconds. Turn to the audience and say: "In a moment Susan is going to mimic uncontrollably exactly what I do with my arms." Turn back to Susan, telling her to keep pressing firmly outward against sides of the door frame until you reach the count of three. At that time she is to stop pressing, relax her arms and walk forward, away from the doorway. Count to three and as she walks slowly forward raise both your arms from your sides until they are almost parallel with your shoulders. Amazingly, Susan will seem to respond almost magnetically to your actions, her arms rising by themselves into the air. She will probably be as surprised as your audience.

What is happening here is that the constant outward pressure has produced a muscular condition which cannot suddenly be reversed by relaxing that pressure. The muscles involuntarily continue to press outward, as they have been conditioned to do, producing the illusion of hypnotic obedience to your suggestion.

THE CHALLENGE

For many years I had a standing offer of fifty thousand dollars to any psychologist, psychiatrist, hypnotist or individual who could prove conclusively the existence of a hypnotic state, a state in which certain phenomena could be produced that could *not* be produced in the absence of such a state. Since the writing of my last book, I was taken to court by a so-called hypnotist who claimed she could prove the existence of such a state and would therefore be entitled to collect the money. Her key witness was a psychiatrist who purportedly induced age regression in a female subject, bringing her back to her childhood. It was, however, pointed out in court that if the woman were really reliving her childhood, as claimed by the psychiatrist, then she would no longer be able to recognize him, as he had played no role in that part of her life! Naturally, I won the case. But justice in the United States of America is not always to be found in the courtrooms. In England and many other countries, the losing party would have been required to pay the court costs, but such was not the case here. It actually cost me more than one hundred thousand dollars in legal fees to hold onto my fifty thousand dollars! Having proved my point in a court of law, I have decided to drop the fifty-thousand-dollar challenge. In its place, I now offer one hundred thousand dollars to anyone who can prove the existence of a hypnotic state! But those accepting the challenge must be prepared to pay all the attendant legal expenses should they fail to prove their case. I am no longer willing to risk the nonhypnotic suggestion that I involuntary hand any more of my hard-earned money to the legal profession!

It is significant that none of the medical "authorities" on hypnosis has ever attempted to challenge my claim. Were they to do so, the "phenomenon" of age regression, which played such a pivotal role in my previous court case, could, no doubt, again be invoked to call into question the entire notion of people remembering better or recalling details more clearly while "under" hypnosis. In the vast majority of cases, I firmly believe that people who supposedly recall hidden information and "suppressed memories" are doing one of two things. Either they are lying, or they are not telling the truth! Over a period of time they may have talked themselves into what they believe to be the truth, but may, in fact, be far from what actually happened. Our childhood memories grow muddled as we age and are rarely accurate and clear. Furthermore, the questions posed by the hypnotist often imply the answers, allowing the subject simply to tell the hypnotist what the latter wants to hear. Finally, hypnotism provides the perfect excuse to reveal information the subject already knew but was too intimidated to reveal under other circumstances, as he or she can later take refuge in the claim that these details were only "remembered" under hypnosis.

I am often asked whether professional hypnotists, psychiatrists or experimental researchers can detect if a subject is merely faking responses and pretending to be hypnotized. My answer, quite simply, is no, certainly not in all cases, even if the researchers or hypnotists are leading professionals with vast experience. The fact that the serial murderer Bianchi was able while hypnotized to convince several expert psychiatrists that he had multiple personalities, when in fact he did not, should prove this point conclusively. Hours of videotapes showing Bianchi in a "hypnotic trance" displaying multiple personalities, were shown as evidence by the defense during his trial. It was only when the expert psychiatrist, Dr. Orne, began to question this diagnosis that the defense contention began to unravel. Orne demonstrated conclusively that Bianchi had faked the entire hypnotic sequence, and so had not even been responding to suggestion at all, a fact Bianchi admitted prior to sentencing. According to Dr. Orne's public statement, it may actually be easier to deceive a professional than a layman when it comes to hypnosis, a fact that—with its frightening legal implications as in the Bianchi case—should haunt the so-called clinical, experimental and medical hypnotists.

Hypnotism is a fascinating area of study. Alas, it has proved to be a great deception, the product of both those who deliberately deceive and those who are themselves deceived in their "findings" about hypnosis.

THE SEALED EYELID STUNT

Among the classic tests of hypnotic influence are the *catalepsies*, in which the subject's muscles are apparently "frozen" rigid by pure suggestion, making it impossible for him or her to bend an arm or unclasp hands. In my performances, both live and on television, I often cause individuals to become immobilized with merely a glance or a quick remark, purely through the legitimate power of suggestion. Sometimes their eyelids become stuck tightly shut under the same influence. Here is a way to use trickery to simulate the latter feat, imitating my legitimate demonstration. This stunt will work with anyone and was, in fact, a favorite of Dr. Harold Rosen, the fear-mongering former head of the American Medical Association's committee on hypnosis. Anyone who took his statements seriously would have believed hypnosis to be extremely dangerous and that stage hypnotists were villains who could force people to commit criminal acts! The ludicrousness of his pronouncements was almost pathetic. Unfortunately, for a while many people, especially professionals, did take him seriously, although today his claims seem patently laughable. Ironically, the following stunt was one of Rosen's pet techniques for testing "hypnosis." Have your subjects seated in front of you, facing the audience and tell them that you are going to cause their eyelids to seal shut so tightly that opening them will become an impossible task. Ask them to close their eyes and imagine there is a hole in the top of their own heads, so large that they can look through it at the ceiling. Instructing them to keep their eyes closed, you say, "Look upward, upward, farther upward, higher and higher, until you are looking at the ceiling through the hole in the top of your head. As you look through this hole, your eyelids will become tightly shut, as though glued together. Keep looking up through the hole, but try to open your eyes, try again, try harder. Now relax. Forget about the hole in your head. Your eyelids are becoming unstuck, the glue is dissolving. Now open your eyes." Your subjects will be as surprised as Dr. Rosen's patients were when he supposedly was introducing them to the hypnotic state. He did not reveal to them how this stunt was done, either because he did not know or chose not to for his own reasons. In any case, suggestion probably had very little to do with your success with this stunt. The fact is that it is virtually physically impossible for someone staring upward with their eyes shut to then open them. Try it yourself. In order to open your eyes you'll need to lower the gaze until it is almost straight ahead. So now you, too, can induce the famous cataleptic stage of the hypnotic trance—by trickery!

THE IMAGINARY INSECT

I have on many occasions demonstrated that the power of suggestion can render an individual not only physically immobilized as simulated above, but that it can actually induce responses to suggestions of a hallucinatory nature, in which the subject sees, hears and, yes, sometimes even feels something that is purely a figment of his or her own imagination. This test will allow you to imitate a "Kreskin hallucination." Your subject will actually feel that some kind of insect is crawling along his or her face, perhaps even entering the ear!

Your audience sees you making a series of "mesmeric passes" in front of the subject, especially around the face. If you have already seen the movie *Mesmer* starring Alan Rickman, for which I served as consultant, then you know that the "father of hypnotism," Franz Anton Mesmer (1734–1815) of Vienna, originally believed in a strange healing power given off by magnets. When he determined that no magnets were necessary for the healing, he attributed the power to himself, claiming to possess an "animal magnetism" that emanated from his hands and body. After Mesmer was forced to leave Vienna, his cult settled in Paris, where no less a scientific authority than our own Benjamin Franklin, then ambassador to the Court of Versailles, helped prove conclusively that there was no such thing as animal magnetism, it being a figment of the subjects' imaginations. But to this day, hypnotists are often caricatured as having such forces coming out of their fingers and eyes, harking back to the original theory of mesmerism. As you make these gestures, your subject will report the sensation that something is indeed hovering around the face and may even try to brush or slap it away.

The secret here is a four- or five-inch piece of stiff black horsehair attached to one of your fingernails. If horses are scarce in your neighborhood, the black synthetic thread used to stiffen sport coats may also be used. Using a small piece of tape, attach the hair or thread to the back of your forefinger so that it extends straight out from the finger. The hair or thread may be longer if its stiffness is sufficient to prevent it from dangling down when the finger points horizontally. If you pay no attention to your hands, neither will anyone else and the hair will pass unnoticed.

Let's assume your subject is a gentleman. When the time for this demonstration arrives, have him close his eyes. Set the stage by suggesting that he is going to feel something moving along the right side of his face, and as you do this, make gestures close to his face with both hands, taking care not to touch him with your hands, but allowing the hair occasionally to brush across the skin on the right side of his face. He will sense this immediately, but with his eyes closed will not be able to discern its true nature. When he reports the sensation, keep suggesting that a bug is flying around, brushing against his face and crawling into his ear. As you make the latter suggestion, the hair should be passing over his ear. Keep your hands in motion and allow the hair to touch the inside of his ear. This will be quite irritating, and when the subject begins to move his hand upward to scratch or slap the bug, move your hands away as you clap them together and tell him the bug is gone, the suggestion is lifted. To your friends, it will look as though you have brought to a dramatic conclusion a Kreskin test of suggestibility.

In previous stunts, in which you simulate some of my demonstrations of the power of suggestion, embroider your presentations with the dramatic hand gestures referred to earlier as mesmeric passes. They will set the stage for this one, making the gestures seem a necessary part of the process and theatrically clouding the true source of the sensation. I often use such gestures in my legitimate demonstrations because they tend to reinforce the suggestions, giving them greater impact. Many modern hypnotists avoid such techniques, feeling they detract from the "scientific" nature of their work by invoking the mysticism of the mesmeric tradition. But the entire hypnotic tradition is, in fact, based on unscientific mystical beliefs, including the belief in a trance state. Since I do not share those beliefs, I regard the use of these gestures as a communications tool. Just as many of my Latin friends use their hands quite expressively to emphasize what they are saying, with my Italian heritage I find it more explicit to express myself using my hands as well as my voice.

IMAGINARY PAIN

In this stunt you will produce an imaginary pain, and this will, in fact, really be more the result of suggestion than trickery. But don't tell your subject that this is a demonstration of the power of suggestion or you'll risk raising the question in the subject's mind of whether what you are saying is real or imaginary, which could greatly diminish or even destroy the impact of the test. Have your subject blindfolded or seated with his or her eyes closed. Announce that you want to administer a test of reflex sensitivity, pointing out that even so sharp a sensation as the sting of a burned match is not usually felt immediately if the subject does not know in advance where the touch will be located. Ask an observer to time the response, which you say will typically be a few seconds after the burned match contacts the skin. At this point, tell your sightless subject to be sure to let you know the instant he or she senses the least discomfort from the heat, as you do not want to inflict any serious pain. Standing very near your subject, light the match, making sure that the sound of it bursting into flames is easily heard, followed by the sound of your blowing the match out. The subject should then feel the matchstick touch the skin. In fact, although the subject really does hear you light the match, really smells the burning wood, and then really hears you blow out the flame, he or she does not really feel the match contact the skin, for you actually touch the subject's hand with the edge of an ice cube. The observers will be amazed at how quickly your subject announces that the pain from the heat of the match is uncomfortable! Such is the power of suggestion!

ANIMAL HYPNOTISM

A few years ago I arranged for an unusual demonstration with a live chicken on my television series from Canada that was broadcast worldwide. I wanted to show the world something that very few people other than farmers seemed to know. The chicken was placed on a table and its head lowered to the tabletop. Starting at the beak, I then drew a chalk line about two or three feet long straight away from the animal. When the chicken's owner let go of it, the bird remained in position as though frozen in place. It was quite remarkable to see, especially in this environment, with cameras moving around, bright lights, a studio audience and there—in the center of everything—an immobilized chicken. It remained there until its owner moved it slightly, at which point the chicken got up and walked around as though nothing extraordinary had taken place. The cause of this phenomenon is not really understood, though one popular theory hypothesizes that the chicken's eyes, lying close to each other and the beak, perceive the line as endless and become transfixed through visual fascination. Until chickens learn to speak, we may well have to be satisfied with such theories, but clearly the chicken is not in a so-called hypnotic trance, a term rendered particularly meaningless here due to the total lack of interspecies communication! In any case, the demonstration does work and has been the source of countless hours of barnyard amusement for centuries.

A similar stunt has been featured on television and in circuses and zoos using alligators. The trainer takes the alligator, holding its jaws tightly shut, and places it on its back. By gently stroking the stomach an immobilizing effect is induced. The alligator will remain on its back, motionless, until disturbed by an outside influence. Having read this, please do not go out and secure an alligator to prove to your friends that you can do a Kreskin! Leave that to the experts and professional animal handlers. But essentially the same technique will work with some common toads and frogs, which you have my permission to "hypnotize."

2
STRONG WORDS

The following tests are designed to impress your audience with your ability to "hypnotize" them, giving them suggestions that render them either weak or strong. The first test you will learn is legitimate. But you will be presenting it as though you have developed special self-hypnotic powers. For many years it was widely believed that hypnotism could be used to endow individuals with greater strength than they would normally be capable of displaying. More recent research shows this not to be the case. Earlier researchers and performers had, in fact, misinterpreted their results. It is now known that, if your concentration is focused on a specific task and you project all your attention, feelings and thoughts in that direction, then you will be able to apply your natural strength with extreme efficiency, sometimes in excess of normal expectations. In fact, in cases of extreme duress, such as a fire or other calamity, the physiological and emotional components may produce adrenaline, which further maximizes the body's strength. There are numerous anecdotal reports of heroic, seemingly superhuman feats by ordinary individuals, such as the lifting of cars off loved ones or the carrying of heavy safes from a burning building. Afterward, under ordinary circumstances, these individuals are often absolutely convinced that they are unable to lift these objects. But under stress, they managed to "forget" their inability and exceed their subsequent expectations. Keep this in mind as you demonstrate the following stunt, which can be presented in the form of a contest with your friends.

OUT ON A LIMB

Tell your friends that Kreskin has developed an advanced form of mental exercise that will allow you to hold your arm out longer than the rest of the group. Ask everyone to stretch an arm out in front of him- or herself and to concentrate on keeping it stiff. You claim that Kreskin's technique allows you to concentrate on your arm with your unconscious mind, freeing your conscious mind for other tasks. To prove this, place a book on your lap and begin to read it to yourself. By keeping your mind on the book, you are actually following the best strategy to win the contest. The others, by concentrating on their arms, will focus on the fatigue and muscle strain they experience, reinforcing it and accelerating its progress. By distracting your attention from the fatigue and ignoring the buildup of muscle tension, you resist that reinforcement and prolong your ability to delay the inevitable. Paradoxically, your lack of concentration is what makes your performance both amazing and possible.

Incidentally, this technique may be applied with equal success to other areas of human interaction, as the reader may well imagine. The Lamaze method of natural child-birth teaches the mother techniques for distracting herself from the pain of labor and in some cases, even chronic pain can be controlled by such an approach.

Often in my performances, perhaps most notably on television, I have given a demonstration that many experts, including hypnotists, believed required a special trance state to accomplish. This is the classic demonstration of catalepsy, in which an individual's body becomes so rigid that it can be placed like a board between two chairs, one supporting the head and the other the feet. The so-called catalepsy is so complete that a large weight placed on the unsupported center of the body will not cause it to sag. I once stood on top of Eddie Albert to demonstrate his rigidity and on another occasion I had Bette Midler sit on Johnny Carson! And neither Eddie nor Johnny (nor Bette, for that matter) was in any kind of special hypnotic trance. There is, however, more to this advanced demonstration than simply distracting the mind, so please do not attempt this yourself. An improper demonstration risks muscle strain and even more serious physical injury.

KNEE HOW, MA?

The following stunt is one of this book's gems. For many years it was a Kreskin exclusive, known to no one else, either in professional entertainment or scientific research. Even though it is based on a unique form of trickery, the late psychiatrist Harold Rosen, who so cherished the eyelid sticking stunt discussed earlier, would surely have used this had he but known of it. It is not discussed in any books on fake hypnosis and I believe it to be original with me. Although I take a certain pride in my discovery, if you have followed my career on television and in person, you will not recall ever having seen me perform this. It has never been a part of my professional presentations. It has never been necessary. Were I to perform such a test, I would do so legitimately. But when you have mastered this presentation, even your subject will be convinced of your mysterious influential abilities. You are going to make it impossible for your volunteer to lift his or her left foot from the floor, or even to bend the leg at the knee!

Let's assume your subject is a gentleman. Ask him to stand with his feet about ten inches apart. He is not to move until you ask him to. Here's how it will look to your subject and the audience: You stand at his right side and reach across and in front of him to brush his left knee with your hand. To do this, you will need to rest your body slightly against his. As you touch his leg, talk about the sensation of the nerves and muscles in it and mention that sometimes the joints can freeze or lock in position. During this discussion, you massage the area above the kneecap and squeeze the knee, so that your subject begins to wonder whether what you are saying might not be true. Incidentally, if you sense that your subject might be uncomfortable were you to touch his leg, simply make mysterious passes and gestures a few inches away from it. Tell him you are actually trying to cause his knee to lock. Tell the volunteer to try to bend his knee and lift his left foot from the floor. Believe it or not, he will be unable to do so. Now reach over and brush his leg upward. Step in front of him, clap your hands and ask him to lift his foot from the floor. To everyone's amazement, including his own, he will do so effortlessly.

Here's the secret behind this original and dramatic stunt: In order to lift his left foot, the subject would have to shift his center of gravity over his right foot by moving his hip to the right. But you are resting (not pressing) against his right side, just enough to prevent this. In taking your initial position, place your left foot almost alongside his right foot, and just before you challenge him to lift his leg, stand with your shoulder and hip almost touching his. Because you are directing all the attention toward his leg, it is unlikely that he will realize what in the world is happening to him.

This test, handled with care, will be something your friends will talk about for some time. Indeed, if you are a medical professional and demonstrate this for your colleagues, they are likely to be as impressed as anyone else, if not more so.

If you doubt the effectiveness of this demonstration, try it on yourself right now. Stand sideways with your right foot against the base of a wall, feet spread about ten inches apart. You will find yourself unable to lift your left foot, for the same reasons just discussed.

HELP, I'VE FALLEN AND I CAN'T GET UP

Let's assume your subject for this is a man. Ask him to lie down on the floor, picking a spot that will not soil

his clothing, preferably on a carpet or rug. You claim that you are now going to use a Kreskin technique to make your influence over the subject so great that he will be rendered helpless, unable even to get up from the floor. Saying you want to strengthen your influence by shutting out all direct light, ask him to close his eyes, and you then cover his face with a handkerchief. Tell the subject to try to rise from the floor. Try though he might and with obvious effort, it will be clear to everyone that he is helplessly immobilized, flat on his back.

The secret of this stunt is something magicians are accused of using almost as routinely as mirrors and their sleeves: a thread! Ironically, it is used here to fake something that I present legitimately on the stage. Sew or tie the ends of a piece of strong thread to the two corners of one side of a handkerchief. The thread, which should be of a color that blends with the handkerchief, needs to be slightly longer than twice the length of one side of the handkerchief, so that when it is firmly attached to the corners it will hang down in the middle to about the center of the handkerchief. The handkerchief is otherwise ordinary and should attract no suspicion. Keep in mind that this is not a trick with a handkerchief, in which you make it vanish or produce something from it. The handkerchief should be seen simply as a convenient way to shut out the light. Once your subject is on the floor, take the handkerchief out of your pocket and hold it by the corners to which the thread is attached. Cover the subject's face by pulling the handkerchief over it, from chin to forehead, taking care that the middle of the thread, which is underneath the handkerchief, comes to rest just under his nose. Still holding the handkerchief by the two corners, pull it just enough to securely engage the thread under the nose. You are kneeling just above the subject's head, apparently just holding the handkerchief lightly over his face. Actually, by controlling the tension in the thread running under his nose, you'll be able to control his mobility! Act for a moment as though some mysterious force were emanating from your arms and wrists, and then ask the subject to try to get up from the floor. As he does so, pull the handkerchief toward the top of his head. This increases the tension on the thread under his nose and the discomfort and pressure it creates will effectively immobilize him in a manner he won't quite understand and will be at a loss to explain later. Each time he tries to get up, as you urge him to do so, maintain the tension until he is forced by the discomfort to recline in frustration. You then announce that you release him from the influence, casually pulling the handkerchief off his face in a downward motion toward his chest. He should have no difficulty rising now, apparently confirming your ability to control his actions through your mental influence.

CHILD'S PLAY

While you can perform the following feats yourself as a demonstration of amazing, Kreskin-like abilities, most are even more effective if performed by a fairly small child nine to twelve years old who is interacting with a fully grown, well-built adult "adversary." The physical contrast in both size and strength dramatizes the suggestions you are pretending to invoke, which could be that the adult will become weaker or that the child will become stronger, or some combination of the two. The child will, of course, have been trained by you to accomplish the feats as outlined below.

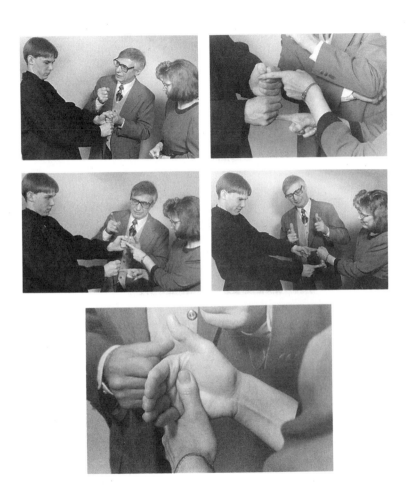

GIVE HER A HAND

Let's assume that your accomplice is a young lady named Lulu. Have her adult counterpart clench his hands into fists and place one fist on top of the other. He is to concentrate on pressing his fists together as firmly as possible. Lulu will then try to separate them using only two fingers. This she accomplishes by extending her forefingers and quickly using them to push his fists in opposite directions. Since he has been pushing down, the unexpected sideways force will meet with little resistance, toppling the two-story tower of fists.

Now it's his turn to try to topple Lulu's fists. But even knowing the technique she just employed, he will continually fail. That is because Lulu has effectively made her two fists a single unit by secretly extending the thumb of her lower fist into her upper fist, which grasps it firmly. No amount of finger pressure will disengage them now.

TAKE A TIP

Now have Lulu separate her fists, holding them side by side and extending her forefingers so that the fingertips touch in front of her. Invite a well-built gentleman to try to pull her fingertips apart. Despite an obvious exertion he will fail to do so until you suggest that his strength is returning, until at last he can gradually separate them.

The secret here is not suggestion, but leverage. Lulu holds her hands together close to her chest and her challenger is instructed to clasp her arms firmly by the wrists and to exert a steady pressure, without jerks or sudden pulls. If he follows your instructions, Lulu will have a tremendous advantage of leverage, making it possible for her to hold out against even the strongest challenger. By having her slowly relax her pressure as you "suggest" the gentleman's strength is returning, you will create a very effective illusion of the power of suggestion.

GETTING AHEAD

Have Lulu place one of her hands flat against the top of her head. You suggest that her hand is becoming so firmly stuck to the top of her head that no one in the audience will be able to lift it off. Those interested in trying are instructed to lift straight up. By concentrating on maintaining the contact between the head and the hand, Lulu can prevent the bond from being broken, since the muscles of each arm are generally sufficiently strong to lift one's own body weight, should it come to that. In fact, this can be taken a step further by having Lulu clasp both hands together and place them palm down against the top of her head. With two gentlemen, one lifting each arm, she will be raised into the air without the mysterious bond being broken.

SUCH NERVE

You now announce that through a combination of suggestion and her knowledge of anatomy, Lulu will render the strongest man unable to lift her from the floor, despite her small frame and light weight. She will be pressing on a special nerve, you claim, rendering the gentleman powerless to lift her. First, have the man clasp Lulu around the waist and lift her from the floor, proving his ability to do so without strain under ordinary circumstances. Now have Lulu find the "special nerve" and press on it as he attempts to lift her again. She carefully places her extended forefinger against the man's chin and presses back on it firmly, as you instruct the gentleman to try the lift again. Despite every effort, he will be unable to do so. This is because Lulu, by maintaining a firm pressure against his chin, can keep him from bending forward to obtain the necessary leverage. She shouldn't push his head back so far as to make the principle obvious, just enough to keep him slightly off balance.

HAVE A SEAT

Have a subject, preferably a skeptical male, sit in a chair, arms folded, legs outstretched and leaning well back. The small of his back should not be in contact with the back of the chair, but away from it as though he were slouched backward.

Now, in your most impressive voice, "command" him to "relax," as though you were actually "hypnotizing" him. Tell him to lean back and make himself comfortable, keeping his arms folded. Now this is important: Have him drop his head back so he can look at the ceiling. When he does this, tell him that Lulu is going to find the focal point on his forehead known as the "third eye," used by Eastern mystics to concentrate their attention. Tell him to close his eyes as she presses her index finger against his forehead. Pause dramatically to give the impression of tremendous concentration, then tell him to try to rise from the chair, keeping his arms folded. Tell him he won't be able to do it, no matter how hard he tries, and then tell him to try as hard as he can. As long as she presses down against his forehead, he will find it impossible to stand up. After about ten seconds, say, "All right now, relax. It's all gone, I release you completely." Have Lulu remove her finger from his forehead as you tell him he can rise from the chair now, still keeping his arms folded. In fact, he can and will. If you handle this properly, he will have no idea what really happened.

In fact, what really happened is that Lulu simply kept him off balance! You can prove this to yourself right now as you read my book. Sit in a chair and begin to rise out of it. Notice that the very first thing you must do to get up is to move your head and shoulders forward to bring your center of gravity over your legs. Now, no matter how much strength you have, you cannot get out of your chair unless and until you move your head forward. But if your head is being held back, the strength of your legs pushing against the floor forces you back into the chair. To move the head forward requires the use of the neck muscles as a whole and Lulu prevented the subject from doing this by pressing down against his forehead, counteracting the use of those muscles. By having the subject keep his arms folded, you also prevent him from shifting his arm weight forward. So his folded arms and Lulu's index finger pressure conspire (with a little help from Mother Nature!) to pin the subject to his chair. If you stage this dramatically, using the commanding voice quality of the stage hypnotist, you will create the con-

vincing illusion of having influenced the subject to respond to your "hypnotic" suggestion.

REVERSE TUG-OF-WAR

Here Lulu will pit her strength against the combined force
of four, five, six, ten or even sixteen people! If she is less
than eight or nine years old, the bones of her wrists may
not be sufficiently developed to allow her to use them to
brace herself safely. In that case, wait a year or two and
try this then.

Have Lulu face a wall with her arms fully outstretched,
placing her palms flat against the wall, fingers pointing
up. Now have a dozen or more people line up behind
her, one behind the other. Each person in line should
stretch his or her arms out, placing them against the back
or shoulders of the person directly in front of them. You
suggest that Lulu's arms are becoming so strong and rigid
that no amount of pressure from the line behind her will
force her closer to the wall. Instruct the group to try to
force her to the wall upon the count of three. Count
slowly and impressively, and then watch the fun as they
struggle in vain. Each person effectively acts as a shock
absorber for the person behind him or her, so that the
strength of the group is not compounded, as one might
intuitively think. In fact, Lulu need only be able to resist
the force of the person pushing directly against her,
which she should do with her wrist and not with the
muscles of the hand alone. If you are concerned that she
may not be able to resist a given individual, you might

have him try to push her to the wall on his own, prior to your giving the "suggestion." If she is unable to resist that person, continue with others as you "suggest" she is growing stronger, until you find someone she can resist, then add the others to the lineup. Often the line will crumble at a "weak link," though tiny Lulu remains unmoved, making for a most dramatic and nearly incomprehensible demonstration.

THE FULL BODY LEVITATION

Having demonstrated your ability to strengthen a child and weaken adults, you will find this stunt a fitting and visually arresting climax to a series of such physical feats. You might set the scene by recounting how pioneer psychic investigator Hereward Carrington investigated the phenomenon about to be demonstrated by having all the parties involved standing on a massive scale. In his experiments, the scale registered a net loss of weight at the climax, a fact that continues to defy modern scientific explanation. While many have experimented with this stunt in childhood, point out that children are comparatively light and that you will be using untrained adult volunteers. I have personally demonstrated this feat on television with Regis Philbin and numerous other celebrities. Once I even staged it outdoors in New York, in front of a musical theater off Broadway and Forty-second Street, using as my subject a rather impressive and imposing gentleman, television and Broadway star Jerry Orbach, and as my assistants dancing girls from the chorus of *42nd Street*, in which Jerry was then starring. Here is what you do.

Have someone sit in a chair. It could be you, but I have found it best to use a female subject weighing 130 pounds or less and to orchestrate the proceedings from the sidelines. I will assume that is the case for this description, and that you are using four male volunteers in addition to your seated subject. Have the four men surround the chair and instruct each of them to clasp his hands together, interlacing the fingers, but leaving both forefingers pointing straight ahead. Have one man place his extended forefingers under the woman's left armpit, another place his forefingers under her right armpit, the third gentleman places his forefingers under her left knee, and the fourth gentleman places his under her right knee. Your seated subject should have her hands clasped and resting on her lap. Instruct the four men to lift her. If you give this instruction quickly and casually, the disjointed and nonunified lifting will at best just cause her to wobble from side to side, with nothing of significance happening. Now the stunt begins!

Instruct the entire group of five to take in a deep breath in unison, hold it in, and then exhale it simultaneously. Repeat this breathing sequence in unison a second time. Finally, have them take in a third breath, and as they do, the four gentlemen should gently lift straight up. To everyone's astonishment, the young lady will rise in the air a foot or more, seemingly as light as a feather. But, equally strange, she will seem to take on more weight within a few seconds, forcing the four men to lower her back into the chair! Several effective ways to present this come to mind: as a demonstration of suggestion, making the four gentlemen momentarily stronger than normal, or perhaps as proof of the mysterious powers that can be tapped by properly controlled breathing techniques, as practiced by the holy men of India.

3

IN THE SPIRIT OF FUN

I've always been pleased that the celebration of Halloween has been so thoroughly embraced by so much of the modern world. Despite all our technological advances, we shall always be intrigued by "things that go bump in the night." I, personally, am a great fan of such classic horror stories as *The Picture of Dorian Gray, Dracula* and *Frankenstein*. But the subject of ghosts goes much deeper than pure fiction. Indeed, all the great terror writers, from Nathaniel Hawthorne and Edgar Allan Poe to our own Stephen King, are acutely aware that somewhere in the deepest recesses of our minds lurks the lingering knowledge that quite possibly there exist spirits or forces seemingly beyond the realm of the living. Magicians have traditionally been regarded as debunkers of the séance world, duplicating through trickery some of the strange phenomena reported to occur there. But the question goes far beyond the mere existence of ghosts to the deeper question regarding the existence of any manifestations not yet fully understood, based not on trickery but on unknown or misunderstood forces. In my opinion, there are indeed such phenomena—some of which have occurred to mediums in séances—and they cannot be dismissed as mere trickery. But that's another story!

Over the years I have held séances in many interesting places. At the request of the producers of "A Current Affair," I held a séance at a famous haunted saloon in Kentucky. Viewers saw tables dance violently out of control even though being pushed down by participants. I was reminded of a similar séance I staged on Johnny Carson's "Tonight Show." On that occasion, one of the tables actually flipped over, crashed into Carson's desk, and split along the side! Were these evidence of the supernatural? By no means. Nor do I honestly believe that there were any spirits involved. The energy producing the table manifestations resulted from the collective unconscious will of the sitters around the tables—but that, too, is another story!

Here I am going to teach you how to duplicate through trickery some of the manifestations reported by séance mediums through the years.

THE SPIRIT TOUCH

It is a little-understood fact that, when we are deprived of sight by darkness, our other senses are both heightened and handicapped. The slightest stimuli can be distorted and magnified, until the trivial becomes terrifying. Ghost stories are always more effective around a campfire or in a darkened room with a dying fire.

The first test is best done alone with a single subject. If others are watching, it becomes too much of a joke at the subject's expense. Let's assume your subject for this is a woman. Ask her to sit in a chair that is backed against a wall. You claim this is to make certain there is no one behind her, but in fact it is to prevent her from pulling back her head and opening her eyes prematurely should she become startled. You do not want that to happen, as it will expose your trickery. Instruct her to close her eyes, telling her that you will then lightly place your right forefinger against her left eyelid and your left forefinger lightly against her right eyelid. With your fingers in contact with her eyelids, you will call upon a spirit from the past, asking it to give a sign of its presence. Emphasize to her that she must keep her eyes tightly shut until you withdraw your fingers. Point out that closing the eyes simulates the total darkness of a traditional séance. Almost as soon as her eyes are closed, she will feel a slight tap on her arm or neck. Remove your fingers from her eyelids, holding them an inch or two away and ask her to open her eyes. She does, and you innocently ask if she felt anything. Of course, she did, so you propose to try to take it a step further. Ask her to close her eyes again, and again place your forefingers in contact with her closed eyelids. This time she'll feel a slight cold breeze on the side of her neck. Remove your fingers and ask for her report. You then propose one final attempt. She closes her eyes again and you place your forefingers gently against her eyelids. This time she'll feel something passing through her hair and may be so startled that she tries to open her eyes, in spite of your earlier admonitions and the contact of your forefingers. Prepare to be amazed yourself when you hear her describe her spirit experience to others!

The secret of this stunt is ingeniously simple. When the subject closes her eyes the first time, don't touch the eyelids with the two forefingers, but with the forefinger and middle finger of a single hand, one finger on each eyelid. It will feel to her just as though you were pressing both forefingers against her eyelids, as you claimed, but in fact one hand is entirely free and you use it to touch her very lightly and quickly on the neck or shoulder. Immediately bring your free hand back in front of her eyes, forefinger extended, and simultaneously remove the other fingers from the eyes, curling your middle finger into the palm. Thus, when she opens her eyes, she sees both hands in position, forefingers extended. You ask what happened, and if your secret touch was sufficiently subtle you may be surprised by her response. This helps create greater anticipation and the feeling that something very ethereal is taking place. Now have her close her eyes again. This time you really do place both forefingers against the eyelids, as claimed. She is already expecting something unusual, and you meet that expectation simply by bending over and blowing sharply on the side of her neck, producing the sensation of a cold breeze. This time she can open her eyes as you remove your fingers, since they were where they should have been. This convincingly reinforces the earlier demonstration, as well as setting the stage for the dramatic climax. Position both your forefingers in front of her eyes again, but when she closes them, immediately extend the middle finger of one hand to leave your other hand free when you contact the eyelids. Gently brush your free hand through her hair and im-

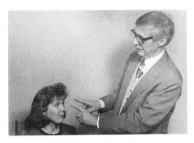

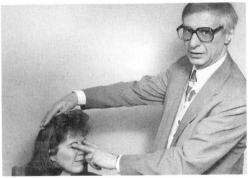

mediately reposition it in front of her eyes, forefinger extended as before. If you are working with an imaginative and suggestible subject, your slight touch, puff of air and movement through her hair will have produced sensations all out of proportion with reality and may well be magnified with each "spirited" retelling!

RAPPING WITH THE SPIRITS

The following demonstration proves the adage that sometimes "less is more" or a little is better than a lot. If

a séance produces large glowing objects and freely float-
ing faces, most sitters rightly assume that they are wit-
nessing a magician's trick, not unlike visiting the Haunted
House at Disney World. But when the phenomenon is
subtle, sitters expand upon it with their imaginations,
creating miracles far beyond the bounds of trickery. The
effectiveness of the secret I am about to share with you
rests entirely on this principle, and was proven time and
again by the fraudulent spirit mediums who used it in a
bygone era.

You and your audience are seated around a table with
your hands on the tabletop, the tips of everyone's little
fingers touching those of their nearest neighbors on each
side so there can be no question that anyone can "break
the circle" by releasing a hand. The lights are turned out
and you begin to await a message or "sign" from the
spirits. Gradually, everyone becomes aware of an eerie
clicking sound which emanates every time you ask for a
communication.

The devilish secret of this stunt demands total silence,
but that is a natural requirement at a séance anyway.
When you form the circle of hands around the tabletop,
with the tips of everyone's little fingers touching those of
their neighbors, make sure that your hands are close
enough for your thumbs to touch. If you have let the
thumbnails grow out a bit, by pressing one nail against
the other as your hands rest on the table you can produce
a click that will be remarkably clear in the silence of the
séance. In fact, as the sitters become attuned to the
sound, they will magnify it in their imaginations. Don't
click your fingernails continuously, perhaps just four or
five clicks every time you ask for a message. When you

ask for the lights to be turned back on, be sure to draw the fingers and thumb of each hand together so that no one will even realize that your thumbs could have come close to one another. Try this and you'll be as surprised by the comments of your audience as they were by the ghostly clicks.

THE PENETRATION OF SOLID THROUGH SOLID

Among the many unusual phenomena reported to have occurred during the turn-of-the-century séances, one of the most striking was the apparent dematerialization and rematerialization of solid objects. Today, one of the most dramatic effects in my own performances elaborates upon this very theme, though it would surely have mystified even the most cynical of mediums. I borrow a number of finger rings from members of my audience, making a point of requesting men's rings or heavy women's rings that will take a bit of a beating. Whether I borrow three, four or five rings, there is always an audible gasp from my audience within thirty seconds after I obtain them, for they see the rings dangling in front of me, linked together to form a simple chain. Most people literally cannot believe their eyes when they see this, so I always insist on handing the rings in this condition to two or three different members of the audience, all of whom incredulously verify that the borrowed rings really are linked. I have performed this in huge auditoriums and even outdoors at state fairs for audiences of more than ten thousand people, and yet everyone seems to comprehend and appreciate the magnitude of the mystery, despite the small size of the properties employed and without the intervention of large-screen televised projections. Although it takes me less than half a minute to link the borrowed rings together today, the very first time I attempted this, at a private party in 1962, it took me nearly fourteen minutes . . . but I ended up with a chain of eighteen rings!

Since I first began performing this, more than thirty years ago, a few performers have tried to simulate it by secretly handing out special rings before their shows and then "borrowing" and "linking" these rings. The rings they use might withstand a cursory inspection, as they appear ordinary, but any jeweler would immediately recognize them as "arthritic rings" that can be snapped open to allow them to pass on and off the deformed fingers of the severely arthritic. As you can imagine, it is relative child's play to link these special rings, once "borrowed."

THE CUFF LINK

Here is a more subtle way to create the illusion of matter passing through matter, in the context of a traditional séance. Tell the group that during the late nineteenth and early twentieth centuries many unusual things were found to occur during spirit séances held in total darkness. Among these manifestations was the decomposition and recomposition of solid objects, including glass and metal. You propose to demonstrate this phenomenon with a large solid ring. The ring, which you will need to supply, must be large enough to fit easily over your hand. An oversize bracelet or an industrial key ring would both work well. Often you can find suitably large brass or wooden rings in specialty shops for decorative purposes. Pass the ring around for examination, so that everyone can make sure it is solid. Seat yourself opposite a subject and then place the ring on your lap. With your left hand, clasp the left wrist of the subject and request that the lights be turned out, but that someone be stationed near the switch to turn them back on in a moment. As soon as the lights are out, you remark to the subject that there would be more control if you were to clasp each other by the fingers rather than the wrists, holding hands in a kind of awkward handshake. You then ask the subject to confirm that your hands are truly locked. Then you take the ring from your lap with your free hand and tap it against the subject's wrist. He or she will confirm this, feeling the tapping quite clearly. You announce that you are going to count to three, at which time you want the lights turned back on, but not before. Call upon the spirits for help and begin your count. When you reach three, call for the lights. When they come on, everyone will see the ring spinning around the subject's wrist, despite the fact that you never let go of his or her hand, as the subject will verify.

The secret here is split-second timing. The moment the lights go out, pick up the ring in your free right hand as you ask the subject to reclasp your left hand at the fingertips. In the moment between the release of the wrist and the regrasping, you seize the opportunity to slip the ring over your left hand and onto its upper wrist. This takes but an instant and in the darkness will pass unnoticed by the subject, who will be concerned with establishing a tight grip at the fingertips, a fact you continue to emphasize. With the grip firmly established and the contact apparently unbroken, you announce that you are picking up the ring from your lap and tapping it against the subject's wrist. Actually, you slide the ring off your wrist and onto the subject's, which you tap with the inside of the ring. With a large enough ring, this is easily done and the subject will confirm your account, being literally in the dark about the actual state of affairs. Just before you call for the lights after counting to three, give the ring a good spin with your free hand as you release it, so that it is seen spinning on the subject's wrist as soon as the lights go on. The subject will find it incredible that the ring passed through his or her arm, while to everyone else it will appear that the ring somehow magically flipped onto the wrist. With a large enough ring this can be made even more effective by making it spin higher on the arm, away from the wrist.

You can follow this by performing the following stunt with the lights on.

A FAMILIAR RING

The secret that I am about to teach you is one of the very oldest in magic, and yet it is still so effective that it can have a tremendous impact on your audience. Tell your friends about my feat of linking borrowed finger rings. You should emphasize the qualitative difference between this feat, with borrowed rings, and the more usual magician's feat known as the "linking rings," in which the performer links special large rings which he provides himself. Tell the group that you are going to attempt a similar feat to mine, but cause the rings to penetrate cords rather than each other. For this, you will need two cords, which can be shoelaces, twine, wrapping string, etc. The important thing is that they be at least twelve to sixteen inches long. Borrow a pencil and tie the cords around it as follows: Drape the centers of the cords over the center of the pencil. Gather both ends of one cord in your left hand and both ends of the other in your right. Tie the double strands in each hand together in a single knot and then hand the resulting left-hand strands to a spectator on the left and the two right-hand strands to a spectator on the right. Borrow two or three finger rings, and perhaps even a bracelet, and thread some over the double strand on the left and the others over the double strand on the right. Ask each of the spectators holding the double strands to hand you either one of the two ends they hold and then tie these ends together into a single knot, ostensibly to secure the rings even more tightly on the cords. What this actually does is exchange the ends of the cords, so that when you hand the end on your left to the spectator on the left, it is the end of the cord that was formerly under the control of the spectator on the right, and similarly for the end now on the right, which you hand to the spectator on the right. If the knots were to dissolve now, each of the assisting spectators would hold the opposite ends of two strands of cord running parallel between them. Ask the spectators to pull on the cords, and as they do, you pull out the pencil, holding your free hand under the rings which appear to be so securely knotted to the cords. Removing the pencil dissolves the knots, freeing the rings, which fall safely into your hand, leaving the cords running between the two spectators, who should be as surprised by this penetration as everyone else.

A HAPPY MEDIUM

Point out to the group that spirit mediums of the past were often tied to a chair or a frame to establish control over their actions and prove that they could not themselves have produced the physical phenomena of the séance room. You'll demonstrate how the ability to dematerialize matter allowed fraudulent mediums to escape such controls. You'll need a piece of soft rope seven or more feet long and a good-size handkerchief or bandanna. Have someone tie your wrists together securely, but not too tightly, with the handkerchief. If the spectator tries to make the binding too tight, simply point out your need to allow your blood to circulate! If you stand sideways with your hands extended, it should be obvious to everyone that your wrists are securely tied together. Have another spectator pass one end of the rope through the circle created by your arms and then pull both ends even, tying the ends into a strong knot and holding onto it tightly. The rope forms a solid ring, linked to the ring formed by your arms and the handkerchief. If you start to back away from the person holding the ends of the rope, you will find your mobility constrained once the rope becomes tight, and yet as you move back and forth and sideways in a kind of gentle tug-of-war with the spectator, you suddenly step back and everyone sees the rope pass from between your wrists and drop to the floor. You have escaped the spectator's control, even though he or she never let go of the rope!

Here's how you do it: As you back away from the spectator who is holding the ends, the rope will be drawn up against the handkerchief. Because the handkerchief is not bound around your wrists too tightly, you should be able to force your hands about half an inch apart at the wrists. When you've done this, begin to rub your wrists carefully together so that they catch the rope between them and begin to work the loop of rope through the center of the handkerchief toward your fingers. Because you are sideways to the audience, they won't be able to see this happening, and even the spectator holding the rope will have his vision of this area masked by the hands themselves. Continue rubbing the wrists to work the loop of rope forward until you can catch the loop with one of your fingers. Use this finger to slip the loop over the hand that is away from the audience. Push your hand through the loop and back away from the spectator holding the rope. This tightens the rope, which will slip off the bound wrists through the handkerchief on the side away from the audience and fall onto the floor. Turn immediately to face the audience and show your wrists are still firmly tied together. You have duplicated a mediumistic stunt!

TABLE TILTING

The table tilting séances that I have presented on television certainly make for a most dramatic demonstration.

But to produce the phenomenon of tables dancing wildly about the room would require training beyond the scope of this book. However, I can show you how to approximate a portion of such a feat, by trickery.

Gather a group around a fairly large card table, perhaps even one weighing several pounds. Have everyone establish a séance circle by placing their hands flat on the tabletop near its edge, with neighboring little fingers touching firmly. In other words, your left little finger will be in contact with the right little finger of your neighbor to the left, and so on all the way around the table, forming an unbroken circle. You can do this with as few as four people, one on each side, although your hands will need to be fairly far apart in order to make contact. If more people are available, encourage their participation, even if it means seating them at the corners if the table is square. You will want the lights low to help create the proper mood, but you do not by any means want total darkness. The tabletop should be clearly visible, as should the hands resting flat upon it. You now ask that the spirits join the gathering to produce the kind of activity that Kreskin demonstrates when he brings tables to life. Sooner or later, someone will mention having felt a slight motion of the table. Then someone will detect slight jerkings or vibrations. Next, it will look as though the table is starting to move slightly and then, lo and behold, one side of the table will start to come off the floor, perhaps rising a foot or more. The other side of the table may even come up, possibly even two sides at once. Finally, the table will come down with a thump and come to rest in "dead" silence. Everyone will breathe a sigh of relief and may well feel slightly shaken.

The secret here is also ingenious and was in fact used by the fraudulent spirit mediums of yesteryear. You will need to wear a full jacket, which can be a sport coat or a jogging jacket, the important thing being that the sleeves extend all the way to your wrists. For once the secret really is "up your sleeves." What they conceal is a ruler or a rod tied to the underside of each arm. The ruler should only extend to within a few inches of your wrist, the area where you would normally have your pulse taken. The ruler should be securely tied about halfway up the forearm. When you rest your hands on the table-top, you will move the wrist forward until the ruler catches the underside of your edge of the table. It need not catch more than a few inches of the edge, as long as it grips it. If you were to lift the table immediately, every-one would look at you with suspicion, but by just lifting slightly, without even bringing the legs up, only the vi-brations will be felt. As more and more people report feel-ing this sensation, begin to lift the table extremely slowly until the legs on your side are off the floor by perhaps an inch. A little is more effective than a lot. In many séance demonstrations people will swear they felt the table rise much more than it actually did, after it has come back down. Ultimately, you can lift the table so that it is per-haps a foot off the ground on your side. Here is a little-known fact that eluded most of the fraudulent mediums of the past: The movement of the table is not limited to your side coming up. If you apply downward pressure on the table with one hand while lifting with the other, you can cause the side of the table adjacent to the lifting hand to come up. For example, if you lift with the right hand and press down with the left, the people on the right will find the table lifting in front of them, a remarkable experience. If, when this starts to happen, you then lift with your other hand as well, your side of the table will come up, leaving the table supported on the floor by only one leg. This incredible phenomenon will be excitedly reported by everyone. When you then let the table lunge down by firmly and rapidly pushing it to the floor, everyone will be shocked. The demonstration is over. Don't yield to the temptation to go any further. Let the participants examine the table and think about their experience.

One final thought: If you really want to boggle minds, have a friend at the other end of the table who is also outfitted with rulers under his jacket. With both of you lifting, the table would ultimately come off the floor entirely, creating the sensation of a spirit levitation. But remember, you don't really need a confederate. Performed effectively in semidarkness, everyone's imagination will embellish the experience almost beyond recognition. Happy hauntings!

4

AND THE BLIND SHALL LEAD THEM

Over the years I've demonstrated some rather dramatic experiments while genuinely blindfolded. Inevitably, the naysayers have conjectured that somehow, through some subterfuge, I can peek out despite the precautions of experts. Some of these self-styled authorities, usually misguided amateur magicians, have gone so far as to claim that it is impossible for anyone to blindfold me completely and that there will always be a way for me to see out, thanks to a tiny tunnel along the bridge of my nose! Would it were so easy! At the risk of sermonizing, let me state my opinion as both a student and *aficionado* of the venerable art of magic, that these overeager hobbyists have always been the worst enemies of conjuring. By overexposing certain principles they have completely corrupted their credibility. In any case, should anyone wish to challenge me, I am quite prepared to prove conclusively my ability to perform some of my most challenging tests while genuinely and securely blindfolded.

CHECKMATE

As a case in point, consider my blindfold chess challenge of Karpov and Korchnoi a few years back. As you may recall, Karpov and Korchnoi were bitter chess rivals vying for the world championship title. It was a classic confrontation: Korchnoi, the Soviet defector, versus Karpov, the Soviet champion. Much of the media attention became focused on Korchnoi's accusation that the Soviets were using a hypnotist to break his concentration. And, in fact, the Soviets did place a prominent Russian hypnotist in the front row of the tournament audience. This was, of course, a classic example of one-upmanship, designed to throw Korchnoi off balance, which it did most effectively. Years earlier Jimmy Grippo, the legendary magician, card manipulator and hypnotist, was similarly retained by several prizefighters to "psyche out" their opponents. He would stand at ringside, staring intensely at the other fighter, supposedly "zapping" him with his "hypnotic powers." In any case, I decided to challenge both Korchnoi and Karpov when their tournament was over. I would play both of them simultaneously and blindfolded to boot! A prominent Olympic chess coach who had helped train Bobby Fischer announced publicly that I was just talking through my hat and that if I did go through with it he would eat his! To everyone's surprise, both Korchnoi and Karpov accepted my challenge and agreed to the tournament. Unfortunately, Karpov had already returned to the Soviet Union and was unable to obtain a travel visa to return to New York, while Korchnoi, the defector, clearly could not go to Moscow. Fortunately, the chess columnist for *The New York*

Times agreed to stand in for Karpov, confident of his proven ability to play a half dozen or more games simultaneously. Now picture me, sitting in the United Nations Plaza Hotel with an audience that included some of the world's most famous chess officials and television crews from around the world, and I was supposed to take on two of the world's leading chess experts while blindfolded! An eye surgeon was brought in to provide the blindfold. She had devised and tested a method of blindfolding herself securely, and she applied this same blindfolding method to me. Now let me point out that I did not expect to win both games under these conditions. Having only played chess a half dozen times in my life, I was simply hoping to hold my own for a respectable period of time. In fact, I found out later that Korchnoi had wagered that the contest would be over in under ten minutes. More than an hour later, I was still playing both men, although all I could do was announce my moves, being unable to see either board. Ultimately, I announced a move and lost to Korchnoi. At that moment he jumped up and ran to the back of the room, announcing that he knew how I had done it. He spoke with Mark Finston, a fine feature writer for the *Newark Star Ledger* in New Jersey, telling him, "Kreskin is reading my thoughts, because I keep thinking. I wrote a note to you saying that if Kreskin castled at this point, he would lose the game, and that's just what happened." Of course, Korchnoi was right. Chess players constantly analyze the board, thinking several moves ahead, anticipating their opponents' best moves. By taking advantage of this, I was able to get the players to play against themselves, until Korchnoi deliberately concentrated on a losing move for me! Incidentally, though I never did have the pleasure of seeing Bobby Fischer's coach eat his hat and though I did not win either game, the one against the chess columnist for the *New York Times* ran nearly two hours!

BLINDFOLD BASICS

Often in my concert performances, I will be blindfolded and have a balloon tossed into the audience where it gets bounced among the thousands of spectators until finally it comes to rest at a random location. With a subject walking close behind me concentrating on the location of the balloon, I will make my way blindfolded through the audience until I finally break the balloon with a needle. Let me show you two methods for simulating such a test through trickery.

1. Take a handkerchief and roll two diagonally opposite corners toward each other until they meet in the center. If you hold this up to the light, it will be obvious to people in front of it that no light is passing through, but if you put this handkerchief over your eyes with the rolls facing you, the space between them will part slightly, leaving you looking through a single piece of fabric. In many cases, if the room is well lit, this will be enough to give you a good view of your surroundings.

2. An alternative method is simply to take a handkerchief and fold it into a thick, opaque bundle which you tie behind your head so that it covers your eyes. The thickness of the handkerchief will prevent you from looking straight ahead, but if you look down, you'll be able to see the floor through the gaps between the handkerchief and the sides of your nose. This is the traditional "magician's peek."

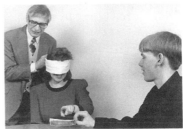

Here's how you can use these methods to convince your friends of your Kreskin-like abilities: Leave the room and have one of your friends hide among the others. While this is happening, you are being blindfolded outside the room. When you are led back inside, you pretend to pick up on the thoughts of the audience, leading you to your friend, whom you tap on the shoulder. Obviously, this will present no difficulty if you can see straight ahead, as in the first method. But what if your sight is limited to the downward peek? Tipping your head back would make it obvious that you are peeking along your nose. The secret is to make a mental note of the kind of shoe your friend is wearing. Then, as you walk through the group, look for the shoes, and tap your friend on the shoulder. You will stun your audience!

PSYCHOMETRY

Some people claim that by touching an object or holding their hands near it, they can get an impression or vibration that will tell them about the object and the people associated with it. In psychic circles this is called psychometry. You can simulate this paranormal claim by using either of the above blindfold techniques. Have people come forward and hold an object in front of you. You hold both your hands about a foot apart and ask that the object be held in the space between your hands. If you are using the nose peek, simply hold your hands so that you can see between them. When the object comes into view, describe its color, shape, function, and so on, as though picking up its vibrations, producing a very dramatic imitation of psychometry.

EST (EXTRA-SENSITIZED TASTE)

During my performances, my sense of hearing seems to become extraordinarily acute. My show business friends and colleagues have often commented on this. I may have picked up a whispered conversation taking place at the other end of a television studio during a rehearsal or camera placement. I am not by nature an eavesdropper, and this tendency for my senses to become more acute even prior to my performances can have its downside: If the background music is even slightly higher than a few decibels, the result for me is often a severe headache.

You can simulate an increased sensitivity of another sense—your sense of taste—by taking advantage of your ability to see downward with a simple handkerchief blindfold. You'll need an assortment of gummed stamps, ranging in value from a few pennies to the more expensive airmail issues. You may even wish to include a few foreign stamps to make the test more interesting. In any case, make sure you have at least a half dozen different values. After you are blindfolded, have the stamps mixed by a spectator, who then selects and hands you one. Lick the stamp and set it aside as you move your tongue around in your mouth as though savoring and analyzing the flavor. Announce the exact value of the stamp and ask for another one, to repeat the demonstration. Each time you do this, don't neglect to spend a few seconds "analyzing" the taste. This will intrigue your audience and make them wonder just what it is about the flavor of the stamps that makes them different. Actually, the differences are on the faces of the stamps, not the backs. As you bring the stamp to your mouth to lick the back, you are in a perfect position to see its face by looking down the sides of your nose. "Handled with care," this feat will be rated "first class" by your friends!

ON THE FINGERS OF ONE HAND

If anyone suggests you can see down the sides of your blindfold, use the following test to "disprove" that hypothesis. Keeping your blindfold on, have a paper bag placed over your head. It will now be obvious to all that you cannot see out, since the bag can cover your shoulders and extend as far down as your upper chest. Call two spectators by name and ask them to come forward. Ask each to think of a number from zero to five and then hold up the corresponding number of fingers on one hand, the closed fist representing zero. A third volunteer is asked to add the two numbers together silently and announce the total out loud. As soon as you hear the total, you are able to state the number of fingers each person is holding up, and you will be correct, not only the first time, but each time you repeat this. Of the two spectators, one will be quite amazed by your ability, while the other will need to act amazed, because that person is your secret accomplice who makes the feat possible.

In the vaudeville era, so-called mind reading acts usually involved two people having a secret system of signals, either a verbal code or a silent, physical means of transmitting information. In this case you do not need signals, but use the "one ahead" principle to know in advance the number of fingers your accomplice will be holding up. Here's how it works: To explain the procedure to your assistants, you do a preliminary run-through. Have each think of a number and hold up the corresponding number of fingers. Ask how many each is holding up, then explain that the third spectator is to add these two numbers together and announce the total, which you demonstrate in this case. Now the test is ready to begin, but both you and your accomplice have noted the number of fingers the first spectator held up during the run-through. This is the number of fingers your accomplice will hold up during the first "real" test. Let's say the first spectator held up three fingers and on the first real test the total announced by the third volunteer is four. Knowing that your accomplice is now holding up three fingers, you can instantly state that the first spectator is holding up only one finger and the second, three. You now know that for the next test your accomplice will only be holding up one finger and so can repeat the test with a different, but equally correct, result. Repeating the test three or four times should be sufficient to convince your challenger that your abilities do not require any vision, without making the pattern of your accomplice's numbers apparent to the group. A slightly more involved method would have your accomplice hold up an apparently random, but actually predetermined number of fingers each time, following an easily remembered pattern (3-5-1 or 4-2-3, for example), then switch to mimic the other spectator once the pattern is exhausted. By using two different methods, it will be impossible for the others to reconstruct even a long demonstration.

Obviously, some of the above tests depend for their effectiveness on the audience believing you cannot see, when in fact you can. But don't let this knowledge blind you to the existence of legitimate tests with secure blindfolds. I am personally prepared to prove for a committee of scientists and journalists that many of my tests can be accomplished legitimately with a total lack of vision. In fact, for some of the most challenging tests, I *require* total blindness to succeed. My chess challenge is a good example of this. Ignoring the expert efforts of the eye surgeon, how would my ability to see have helped me in my contest with these two chess champions? In fact, the exact opposite was true: Had I *not* been genuinely blindfolded, I probably would have lost both games in a matter of minutes, as predicted by Korchnoi. The television lights and crews, the media circus, the intimidating crowd, all these would have conspired against my ability to concentrate. Filtered out by the blindfold, I was able to pit the players against themselves. And therein lies the real secret of my work with blindfolds!

KUDA BUX

Some years ago a fascinating figure from India created a sensation in the Western world. He initially gained prominence by walking across a bed of hot coals in a demonstration in England in 1935. He staged a similar fire walk for Robert ("Believe It or Not") Ripley in Rockefeller Plaza in New York three years later. On that occasion even he found the coals uncomfortably hot and had to rush through his walk. His name was Kuda Bux, a genuine man of mystery whose entire career was really based on "sightless vision," the ability to accomplish incredible feats while blindfolded. Since his death in 1981, a number of Kuda Bux "wannabes" have claimed they knew how he did this. I think I am safe in saying that these second- and third-rate magicians are either deluding themselves or just plain lying. To this day, no one has ever succeeded in presenting Kuda Bux's demonstration as he did it. In fact, his ability was not based on telepathic skills, but on another highly developed sense, a fact apparently unknown to his imitators. Even Kuda Bux's son has stated publicly that he has no idea how his father accomplished his feats of sightless vision.

Perhaps Kuda Bux succeeded where Houdini failed and actually carried his secret with him to the grave. At times he suggested that his vision was made possible through the skin and pores left uncovered by the massive blindfold engulfing his head. His hands and neck were both left exposed and perhaps, as he suggested, this may have enabled him to see in some unorthodox way. Once, during a private demonstration, someone turned out the lights of the room in which he was being tested and Kuda Bux was unable to function. Paradoxically, although Bux's eyesight became weak in his later years, his demonstrations of eyeless vision continued unimpaired.

In my own case, I have never claimed that I could "see" without the use of my normal vision. It is true that I can perceive certain things, but only through the agency of another individual acting as a sender. In classic thought-reading experiments there is always a sender and a receiver, the latter being the individual attempting to pick up the thoughts of the sender. Obviously, if the sender were placed in darkness, it would be impossible for me to accomplish certain tasks. But there are many ways a sender can concentrate on an image and this very fact has allowed me to give demonstrations and performances for audiences consisting almost entirely of those who are sightless, as well as audiences of those unable to hear. In both cases I have always found individuals whose heightened abilities in the use of their other senses have made the challenge of my role as receiver a particular pleasure.

5

FUTURE FORETOLD

Although I have not made it my specialty, on several occasions throughout my career I have attempted to project my thoughts and feelings to the point of anticipating the results of some future event. Years ago, when Medicare was first introduced into Congress, I attempted to analyze the forthcoming vote and actually succeeded in predicting the outcome within one or two votes, more precisely than the professional pollsters, garnering considerable attention.

More recently, CNN has asked me on two occasions to predict the winners of the top twelve categories of the Academy Awards. The first time, I not only succeeded, but in one case even surprised myself! I had been unable to pinpoint which movie would win in the "Best Foreign Film" category and so had to be satisfied with narrowing it down to only two choices. As it turned out, the Academy that year had also been unable to decide and ultimately gave Oscars to both the films that I had named!

When CNN asked me to repeat the analysis the following year, I declined to go so far again, pointing out that it had taken me more than thirty hours of solid research the previous year, reading reviews from various critics, analyzing them and reflecting on the state of the Academy, not to mention trying to see as many of the films as possible myself! Instead, I offered to make predictions about the ceremony. Unfortunately, I was performing onstage in Indianapolis, Indiana, at the very time the Academy Awards were being televised that year, so I was frustrated not to be able to watch the proceedings. But I pointed out to my live audience that one of my predictions had involved an onstage accident in which someone's trousers would be ripped. When the prediction, which had been sealed and given to an official a few days earlier, was opened and read on a CNN newscast the next day, I was able to credit myself with some success. Although no one's trousers were literally ripped, one of the presenters, accident-prone comedian Chevy Chase, walked out and dropped his trousers to get a laugh. In this case, the significance of my prediction only became obvious after the fact.

EXACTLY THE SAME

Now let me show you how you can, through trickery, imitate a Kreskin prediction and create quite an impact on your circle of friends. But make sure that you have a gathering of at least a dozen people when you try this and have your prediction written out, folded up and sealed in an envelope, and placed in a conspicuous and tamper-proof location when your friends arrive. It might be in a small chest on a table or in a cigarette box on a dresser or even taped to a door. Point out to your friends that it contains a very special prediction, obtained by methods you learned from Kreskin.

Now for the buildup. Save the prediction for last, performing some of the other stunts from this book first and then announcing that you will end the demonstration by revealing your prediction of something that is about to happen. Ask one of the spectators to go over to your bookshelf or coffee table and pick any one of the books or magazines there. Have him or her examine it carefully and then secretly pick out some phrase in it. Hand the spectator a notepad to write down the phrase. The spectator can even leave the room with the book and pad to do this. Once it has been done, have another spectator, preferably one who does not know the first spectator well, retrieve and unseal your envelope, removing the prediction, but not unfolding or revealing it yet.

You now ask the first spectator to read aloud the phrase that he or she freely selected from all the books and magazines available. Have it read aloud a second time. Finally, ask the other assisting spectator to open your prediction and read it. He or she will announce that it says exactly the same sentence! Try to imagine how stunned your friends will be. Perhaps you really do have the gifts you claim, or have somehow developed and are exhibiting the inherent abilities that I demonstrate. It would be a mistake at this point for you to reveal to the group how you did this. Not only would you suffer a loss of prestige, but it would probably make them feel foolish and let down to have been deceived by such a simple trick.

There is one other person who knows what really happened, however, and that is the spectator who opened and read your prediction.

Let's review the final sequence: The first spectator reads aloud the secretly chosen phrase and you immediately ask that it be read aloud again, as though firmly establishing it in everyone's mind. You then have the second spectator, who retrieved the prediction and is now standing beside you, open your prediction and read what it says. He or she will say that it says exactly the same sentence, and as soon as this is said, take back your prediction, giving the assistant a conspiratorial wink with your "upstage" eye, the one that is away from the rest of the audience. You do this because here is what you actually wrote on the paper: "It says exactly the same sentence." Remember, you asked the spectator to open your prediction and read what you wrote. The audience thinks that he or she is reading it silently and then simply confirming the accuracy of your prediction, when, in fact, the person is literally reading what is on the paper, repeating the phrase exactly. If you are clever enough in your handling of this, picking the second spectator carefully and using your wink to let them know it is all in fun, chances are good that your secret is secure for a while and, as far as anyone else will know, you have done a prediction a la Kreskin.

A MENTAL TARGET

One experiment has been featured so often in both my public concerts and on my television appearances that it has practically become identified with me as a signature piece. A partial list of the celebrities who have assisted me with this experiment would include Dick Cavett, Mike Douglas, Regis Philbin and David Letterman. Prior to the performance I peruse a page from a book or a newspaper or even a telephone directory and jot down an impression, which is then sealed in an envelope, both to keep the contents secret and to secure them from tampering. At the appropriate time during the performance, a spectator—often a total stranger—is invited to move his or her finger over the page without looking at it, and then to drop the finger blindly onto it, randomly selecting a word or a name or a number. Sometimes I have them mark the spot with a pen or a pencil, but most often I simply ask them to point to it. Invariably they are pointing to the very word, name or number that had impressed me earlier, the "mental target" I had jotted down and sealed up.

Many have asked me how I do this, and, to be honest, it is difficult for me to explain and impossible to teach. Basically, I influence the unconscious response of the subject. But this process has become so second nature to me that my own mental processes as I do it are themselves largely unconscious. Perhaps it is this very fact that makes this test one of the highlights of my performances.

Even though I can't teach my method, I can show you how others have faked my test, using trickery to simulate my success. Feel free to try it yourself. Get a small, pocket-size magazine, such as *Reader's Digest* or *TV Guide* and a felt-tip marking pen. Open the magazine to a page, show the page to your subject, and then place the open magazine in the subject's hands behind his or her back. The subject is then given the felt-tipped marker and instructed blindly to mark the page with a large X running diagonally across the page from corner to corner. You step back and turn away as this is done. Now tell the subject to bring the book forward and note what word has been randomly chosen by the intersection of the two lines forming the X. Without turning around, you announce the very word. You are correct!

It would, of course, be wonderful if you could influence the subject's unconscious motor skills to cause the line to be drawn by the subject to pinpoint the word precisely. But such is not the case, so here is what you really do: Prior to the demonstration, choose a page in the magazine with no obvious distinguishing features, such as a photograph or a headline, and which immediately follows a similarly undistinguished page. Put the open magazine behind your own back and mark an X on the page with a felt marker. Now bring it forward and memorize the word or phrase at the intersection of the two lines. When you open the magazine to show the subject a page, you actually open it to the page before the marked one, which looks the same, but is unmarked. As you walk behind the subject to place the open magazine behind his or her back, simply thumb over to the next page, bringing the marked one uppermost, the other pages being folded under. Now bring out a felt-tipped marker, remove the cap and hand the marker to the subject with the instructions about blindly marking the page with an X. Although this pen matches the one you used to mark the page yourself, it is, in fact, dry and no longer writes, because you left it uncapped for several days prior to the performance! You can keep this secret by immediately retrieving the marker from the spectator in order to replace the cap, which you still have, and then put the marker in your pocket. Naturally, you will now have no trouble predicting or divining the words "marked" by the spectator, since they are the ones you marked yourself!

6

IT'S IN THE CARDS

When I was about nine years old I began to practice magic tricks. Magic became an obsessive interest and its practice became the focal point of my extracurricular activities, a condition persisting through my teenage years. But even before reaching my teens, I had begun to find that I could accomplish by legitimate means many of the tricks I was working so hard to learn to fake. In other words, I was using genuine abilities to simulate fake ones! With this realization was born my ambition to become a legitimate mentalist.

The following test marked a turning point in my life. For many years I would not discuss it, but I can clearly remember repeating the test time and again for relatives, teachers, classmates and neighbors when I was only nine or ten years old and getting *true results!*

Now you may be wondering why I am including a legitimate test here, since the purpose of this book is not to teach you to become a genuine telepathist or mentalist, but rather to fake what I do in my public performances. Well, for decades people have reported that while faking paranormal activity, they have actually begun to experience genuine phenomena which they could not explain. Naturally, there are those who would like to believe that those people are merely deceiving themselves, but having had this experience myself, I am convinced otherwise and urge you to give this a try. And as your reward, I'll show you afterward how you can simulate it by trickery!

A LEGITIMATE TELEPATHIC TEST

One other person is required for the test and it is best if this is someone with whom you feel a close rapport. Take six to eight cards from a deck and lay them in a random order faceup in a row on the table, spaced about two inches apart. This test can, in fact, be done with the cards facedown, but you will find it easier at the beginning to work with the cards faceup, giving the sender you are working with a clear visual focus on which to concentrate. Ask the other person to think of one of the cards and to let you know when he or she is ready to proceed.

Now, your mood is critically important. Try not to think of anything at all and, in particular, do not try to guess the card on which the sender is concentrating. Hold your hand about three inches above the outer edge of the first card in the row. You can hold it higher, if this is more comfortable, the important thing being that it begins over the first card. You then proceed to move it slowly along the entire row, passing over each card until you have reached the outer edge of the last card in the row. After a brief pause, reverse the procedure, passing your hand over the cards in the opposite direction. Go back and forth several times.

As you continue this process, you will notice that your hand seems to dip over some portion of the row. Don't try to analyze this tendency or rationalize it and especially take care not to exaggerate it. Just let it happen. Countless studies have shown that intellectual reasoning, critical analysis, and conscious skepticism all inhibit telepathic communication. Gradually slow the motion of your hand until you clearly recognize over which card it is dipping. Once you are certain of the card, pick it up and ask your subject if it is the one on which he or she is concentrating. If you are using six cards, your chances of being correct purely by chance are only one in six. If, however, you are beginning to become sensitized to the inclinations of your subject, you will find your success rate will be much, much higher.

Don't be discouraged if you are not successful at first, and don't expect one hundred percent accuracy with every sender with whom you work. Even after many years' experience with this test, I would never expect or claim an accuracy rate of one hundred percent. Incidentally, if your first choice is wrong, ask your subject to concentrate on the card again, actually trying to visualize it, but keeping both eyes open and watching you as you move your hand. You may also wish to try closing your eyes and ask someone else to observe your hand, watching for the slight dipping over a particular card. If you succeed even one-third of the time, you will still be well ahead of the law of averages. As you begin this experiment, you will probably find that when you pick the wrong card, it will be just beside the right one.

If your initial success rate is no better than dictated by chance, there may be several things going on that are worth examining. First, telepathic communication is largely an unconscious activity and you may be over-whelming it with conscious processes. You might also be trying too hard, introducing a tension into the procedure that interferes with your sensitivity. Under stress, you may actually be responding to an autosuggestion regard-ing the choice—in effect reading your own mind, rather than that of your sender. Finally, if your success rate is well below what even chance would dictate, then you may, in fact, be responding to the sender, but consistently misinterpreting the signals. Often this can be remedied by simply making the opposite choices in subsequent tests, countering your intuition to correct its bias.

Regardless of your success rate, don't worry about the results. After all, you're not reading this book to develop genuine ability, but to learn how to fake it!

With that in mind, here's a way you can simulate this test, succeeding without relying on any latent telepathic ability.

AN ILLEGITIMATE TELEPATHIC TEST

Take a deck of cards and have it thoroughly shuffled. Take back the deck and spread it facedown between your hands, inviting a spectator to remove a card from the deck, but to keep it facedown, without looking at it or showing it to anyone until you turn away. Turn your back to the spectator, who is then to look at and remember the card. When he or she has done so, turn around again and have the card replaced somewhere in the middle of the deck. Place the deck on the table and ask the spectator to give the deck one or two straight cuts. Now you spread the cards faceup on the table so they are all visible and begin to pass your hand over the entire spread. It will begin to dip over one card, just as in the genuine test, and when you push a single card forward from the spread, it will be the chosen card.

Here's what you've really done: When your back is to the audience, separate the spread of cards in the center and look at and remember the bottom card of the top half. Holding the spread together, turn around and ask the spectator to replace the chosen card. For convenience you open the spread slightly for the replacement of the card, which places the chosen card directly beneath the card you just looked at and are remembering. Close the spread and square up the deck. Place the cards on the table and have the spectator cut them once or twice. Though the cutting changes the positions of the cards, unlike shuffling, it does not change their relative order, so the card you are remembering will still be immediately above the chosen card, though both will be displaced from their original position. Spread the cards faceup on the table, looking for your card as you do so. The spectator's card will be the one just below it (if your card happens to be the very bottom card of the deck, then the chosen card will be the top card of the deck). Begin to move your hand back and forth over the spread, making sure it dips slightly each time you pass over the chosen card, until finally you touch that card and dramatically push it forward, announcing that it is the chosen card. A simple trick, but one that allows you to simulate a genuine telepathic test.

CARD DIVINATION

You can probably tell that I love a good card trick, especially one that can be done anytime, anywhere. Here is one that will appeal to those of you who play gin rummy, poker, pinochle or hearts, both the latter being two of my favorite games. You can do this with any deck of cards, pinochle or regular, complete or not.

Have the cards shuffled, then spread them faceup on a table so everyone can see that they really are well mixed. Gather up and square the cards, which you place facedown in front of one of the spectators, asking that person to cut the cards somewhere in the center of the deck and to place the two halves side by side on the table. You pick up and look at the top card of one of the heaps and use it to calculate the top card of the other heap, which you then name. Your prediction proves correct and you can repeat the trick a few times with other spectators. When you are ready to bring the trick to a dramatic conclusion, announce in advance that this time you will name the cards on both halves. A spectator cuts the cards and you proceed to name two cards, which are then shown to be the top cards of each packet!

The secret here is so simple that you must take care not to overdo the trick, lest it become obvious. Here's what you do: Following the procedure outlined above, when the deck is spread faceup, ostensibly to show how well shuffled it is, you are really noting and remembering the top card of the deck. The cards are then gathered up and placed in front of the first spectator, who is instructed to cut the deck into two piles. Once he has done so, it is best to introduce a little time delay, asking if he cut them carefully, did he notice how well shuffled the deck was, etc. The purpose of this strategy is to give the audience time to forget which half of the deck came from the top. Pick up and look at the top card of the other half and apparently use it to figure out what the other top card is, really, of course, just naming the card noted earlier. But while you are looking at the top card of the bottom half, take the trouble to memorize it, so that you will be set to repeat the trick simply by making sure that this card ends up on top when the deck is reassembled after your first prediction has been verified. Repeat the trick once or twice with other spectators, then announce that you will attempt something doubly impossible. Tell your friends that this time you will name both top cards, without seeing either of them!

Have the deck cut into two halves. Just as before, you already know the name of the top card of one of the piles. Let's assume it is the ace of spades, and that the other card, which you don't yet know, is the king of hearts. Point to the unknown top card and announce, "This card is the ace of spades . . ." With one hand, pick up the card you just pointed to and look at it as you point with your other hand to the true ace of spades and announce, ". . . and this is the king of hearts!" naming, of course, the card you just looked at. Immediately pick up the ace of spades and place it in the hand with the king of hearts, tossing both faceup onto the table to verify the accuracy of your divination.

A CARD TEST A LA KRESKIN

One reason thought-reading experiments with playing cards have always intrigued my audiences is probably because they can imagine the tremendous advantage such an ability might give them at the gaming tables. Blackjack is the most popular casino card game, but there is, in fact, no real advantage for me to play it in a casino setting because the dealer, whose thoughts I would want to read, is only allowed to peek at his facedown card if his faceup card is a ten or an ace. If he has a blackjack, the game is over and if not, he continues the deal. Since his actions are entirely dictated by the rules of the game, he is unlikely to concentrate on the value of his card, giving his attention instead to the plays in progress.

Unfortunately, without his active concentration, the chances of anyone picking up the value of his hole card from his thoughts are indeed very slim. In recent years, many casinos have eliminated even that possibility by having both the dealer's cards dealt faceup, the second card only being dealt after all the other players have received their final cards. This rule was not established to eliminate any perceived advantage to a thought reader, but was designed to minimize cheating by the dealers themselves. Contrary to popular belief, the dealers, if dishonest, rarely cheat the players, but instead cheat the casinos.

Here is a stunt with playing cards that is quite effective in creating the illusion of telepathy. I used to call it the Latin card trick, because when I learned it as a kid I had to memorize four Latin words. This version will be easier for you to learn because the key words that you'll need to remember are all English. Here's what you do: Deal twenty cards faceup onto the table in ten pairings of two cards each. You may wish to refer to these as blackjack hands and weave a presentation around that theme. Invite three or four people to think of any one of the "hands," remembering both cards of that pair. Pick up all the pairs and deal them faceup onto the table in an apparently haphazard manner, resulting in four rows of five cards each. Actually, the dealing is not haphazard at all, and this is where the key words come into play. The words are *chaff, sheer, usual* and *color.* Note that these four- or five-letter words are constructed from ten different letters of the alphabet, each letter being repeated twice.

As you deal the cards, you will be associating each pair of cards with one of the ten letters. In dealing the cards, simply visualize the four words on the tabletop, then deal each pair of cards onto a corresponding pair of letters. For example, you might deal the top card to the position of the *c* in *chaff* and the second card to the *c* in *color.* The next card could be placed on the *h* in *chaff,* and the following card on the *h* in *sheer,* and so on with each letter and card pair until all the cards are on the table.

Now you must ask each spectator thinking of a card pair to tell you in which rows his or her cards are. With that information, you immediately know the pair. For example, if a spectator is thinking of cards in rows two and three, then the cards correspond to the letter *s,* the only letter common to both rows. If they are both in row four, then they correspond to the letter *o*, the only one repeated in that row. Once you have memorized the four key words and have practiced casually dealing out the ten pairs in the "haphazard" pattern, you'll be ready to pick out the card pairs instantly and with a flourish. Because only you know the key words, it will be almost impossible for your friends to reconstruct your secret.

EYELESS SIGHT

One of my favorite newsstands is run by a man who has been completely blind since birth. First-time customers always marvel at his ability to distinguish a one-dollar bill from a ten or a twenty, apparently by the sense of touch alone. In my performances, I try to take this remarkable skill a step further by describing objects such as playing cards that are held not only out of sight, but often well beyond the range of my touch by members of the audience. The playing cards and other objects are always supplied by the corporation engaging my services, to preclude the obvious suspicion of prearrangement. Here is a way for you to imitate a demonstration of "eyeless sight" or paroptic vision, using a method so diabolically clever that it will even mystify most self-styled "magicians."

The audience sees you take a deck of cards, shuffle it, and drop it into an ordinary but completely opaque paper shopping bag. Have someone hold the bag tightly shut and shake it vigorously to mix the cards even more. The spectators then blindfold you as thoroughly as they wish, and when they have done so you reach inside the bag, bringing out single cards, each of which you unhesitatingly name. After doing this two or three times, you take it a step further by naming one or two cards even before your hand emerges from the bag. As a climax to the demonstration, you name a card, reach into the bag and, after a brief search, triumphantly remove that very card!

Would you believe the secret is a paper clip? That's right! Pick six or seven cards that you want to use for this demonstration, place them in an order you have memorized and paper clip them together at one end. Add this paper-clipped "stack" to the bottom of the rest of the deck and place the deck in the card case. With a little practice and experimentation, you will find that you can easily hide the paper clip with your fingers as you remove the deck from the case and give the cards a quick overhand shuffle, which will also not disturb the paper-clipped cards. Drop the cards in the bag and have someone shake it while you are being blindfolded. If the paper clip is a good one, the shaking will not remove it from the small batch of cards. Now it is a simple matter to reach inside and find the paper-clipped cards. Of course, you should have noted which side of the batch the short arm of the paper clip was on, allowing you to tell by touch the top of the batch from the bottom (or you can place a bend in the paper clip to make this even more obvious). Now all you need is a little acting ability to make it seem as though you are sensing the cards as you merely recite your memorized stack. And be sure to spend some time "searching" for the final card before bringing it out. Skeptics in your audience will probably accuse you of using Braille playing cards, but the beauty of this method is that although the cards really were "marked" (with the paper clip), at the end you finish "clean" and everything can be examined.

KRESKIN — UNDER THE TABLE

Here is a similar stunt, more appropriate for less formal settings. It uses playing cards again to simulate a test I have often performed during interviews and at small gatherings in which I describe objects being held out of sight under a table. I don't bother with a blindfold for this, since it is obvious that no one, including myself, can see what is being held under the table.

I recommend that you use an old, well-worn deck for this, for reasons that will be obvious in a moment. Hold the cards out of sight under the table and ask the person seated across from you to reach under the table, remove any card from the deck and then carefully move it to his or her edge of the table to see which one it is, taking care that no one else can see the card, or even its back, to eliminate the possible suspicion of "marked" cards. Once the identity of the card has been noted, have it replaced in the deck, still held beneath the table. As the card is replaced, squeeze the deck tightly at the end nearest you, which prevents the card from being inserted completely into the deck. Pull back the deck slightly and—assuming that the deck is being held facedown—tear off the outer right corner of the protruding selected card. This is one of the index corners (if the deck is faceup, tear off the outer left corner). Immediately push the rest of the card into the deck, which you then hand to the spectator to shuffle under the table. As this is being done, you need only glance down at the corner in your hand to know which card was selected. When you name the card cor-

rectly, the surprise will almost certainly overshadow any desire on the spectator's part to examine the cards, especially if you are using a borrowed deck.

THE KRESKIN BLINDFOLD DECK

You've learned how to identify cards when you are blindfolded, and when the cards are held out of sight under a table, but what if the cards themselves are blindfolded? Here's what you do: Have someone take and shuffle a borrowed deck. As this is being done, spread a handkerchief flat on the table and ask that the shuffled deck be placed facedown on the center of the handkerchief. You then proceed to wrap the deck in the handkerchief, but as you first turn the deck in winding it up, you will find that if the single layer of the handkerchief covering the bottom is drawn tightly against the bottom card, the cloth will be thin enough to see through, revealing that card. Don't hesitate as you glimpse it, but continue to wrap up the deck until it really forms an opaque bundle, which you hand to a spectator for safekeeping. Dramatically rub your hand along the bottom of the bundle, announcing that you can "sense" the card. Name the card and then allow the spectator to unwrap the deck and reveal the card, confirming the accuracy of your "senses."

SEEING RED

For many years it was widely believed that a deep hypnotic trance was necessary to induce hallucinations in a subject. As I routinely demonstrate in my performances, people can be induced to see birds, rabbits, UFOs and other figments of their own imaginations, purely through the power of suggestion, without benefit of the so-called trance state.

In discussing my demonstrations, people will begin to wonder whether you can somehow make them see colors through suggestion, so here is a way for you to simulate such a hallucination, without even needing the power of suggestion. The audience will see you take a deck of cards, hold it at one end, and riffle the top of the deck in front of a spectator's eyes. This spectator will say that all the cards are red. You smile and, as you move with the deck to another spectator, suggest that perhaps this is because you removed all the black cards beforehand. Riffle the cards before a second spectator's eyes and ask whether the cards are still all red. This spectator will say that, instead, they are all black! You act surprised and show everyone that the face card of the deck is, in fact, a joker, which is neither red nor black. Finally, you riffle the cards before a third spectator, whom you ask to "break the tie," telling everyone whether the cards are red or black. In this case, diplomacy prevails, for the response is resoundingly "both!" In fact, you can now hand the cards out for inspection, and they prove to be an ordinary and complete deck of cards. Were the first two spectators hallucinating?

Thanks to some clever advance preparation, they were, in fact, being totally candid in their responses, without being under the influence of any suggestions. Divide the deck into the red and black cards and set aside the joker. Place a red card on the table, then a black card on top of it, but offset so that it projects about an inch below the end of the red card. Then place a red card on top of this, but aligned with the first red card. Alternate the red and black cards, so that the red cards project about an inch at one end and the black cards project about an inch at the other. Carefully push the two projecting halves closer together until the deck is almost, but not quite, squared up. Place the joker on the face of this deck and you are ready for the demonstration. From a few feet away, the deck looks ordinary, but because the cards are not squared, when you hold the deck firmly at one end and riffle the other end by pulling back on it with the thumb of your other hand, allowing the cards to spring off your thumb, only one color will be seen. This is because you are only riffling the colors that protrude. As you proceed to the second spectator, turn the deck around in your hand and riffle the other end, displaying the other color. As you proceed to the third spectator, push the cards flush, squaring the deck, so that both red and black are seen when you riffle the cards. While you can now hand the deck out for examination, I would recommend giving it a quick shuffle first, to break up the alternating pattern of the colors. Otherwise someone might gain a clue to the secret of this amazing feat and it is just too good to let that happen. Remember to keep the secrets of your demonstrations secret. Otherwise your prestige will suffer irreversible damage, as most people simply do not appreciate such clever, but often simple, ideas, preferring instead to fantasize about mysterious powers.

7

SUNDRY STUNTS

KRESKIN'S ONE IN A MILLION

In my annual concert appearances in theaters, stadiums and nightclubs around the world, I often feature a brief interlude that many consider to be a substantive and conclusive test.

During my recent performances headlining at the Debbie Reynolds Theater in Las Vegas, many prominent magicians attended and singled out this test as one of the most convincing, since it is clearly beyond all possible trickery. But I'll show how you can fake it, by cheating!

Basically, I have members of the audience jot down simple thoughts which they then fold up and drop into a bowl or onto a plate. These thoughts are typically contributed by one-half of the audience members, if not more. I then walk up to a total stranger and have that individual take any one of the slips. He is then to concentrate on that thought and my task is to try to perceive it. This is much more difficult than when I sit on stage and tune in to the barrage of mental images that are being simultaneously transmitted to me by members of the audience. In the latter case I simply pick up the very strongest impressions. But in this case, I am committed to zeroing in on the specific thought of a single individual.

Here's how you can imitate my "One in a Million" test of thought perception: You'll need a writing pad with fairly small sheets and a bowl. Instead of having your friends jot down a thought, ask each of them to call out a three-digit number. You repeat the number and write it down on a slip of paper, which you then fold twice and drop into the bowl. This is repeated for each number called out, with all the pieces folded identically so you cannot be accused of marking the slips to keep track of them. When each person has named a number (and with a small group, you can have each person name several numbers, going around the group more than once), hand someone the bowl and ask him or her to mix up the slips and then pick one out of the bowl. Take back the bowl, walk away and ask the spectator with the slip to open it up and silently read the number on the paper, without revealing it to anyone else. After concentrating for a moment, you pause dramatically and then announce a number, which proves to be the one the spectator was thinking of, as can be verified by passing the slip of paper around the group.

Unless you have developed the abilities that I demonstrate throughout the world, you will need to cheat for this test to succeed every time. Here's how you do it: Let's say the first number called out is 351. Repeat it, write it down, fold up the paper and drop it into the bowl. Let's say the next person calls out 732. Repeat it, write 351, the original number, on the paper, fold it and drop it in the bowl. No matter what numbers are called out, repeat them aloud, but always write the first number, 351, on the slips. Ultimately, you will have a bowl filled with identical folded slips each bearing the number 351!

Once the spectator has mixed the slips and removed one of them from the bowl, take back the bowl and move away from the spectator. Apparently you are doing this to avoid seeing the number on the chosen slip, but really you are getting the bowl (with its incriminating evidence!) away from the center of attention. After you

have revealed the number, you can keep the heat off the bowl by focusing attention on the slip of paper that is being passed around. Don't sell this stunt short. If you take it seriously and keep your cool, your friends will credit you with Kreskin-like powers!

KRESKIN'S MASS AUDIENCE PROJECTION

In most of my concerts I demonstrate the ability to influence a mass audience by attempting the mental projection of a single thought—be it a name, number, scene or feeling—to everyone attending my program. On occasion, as many as six and even seven thousand people have succeeded in picking up the very thought that I was projecting. Let me show you two ways to simulate the Kreskin Mass Audience Projection Test, creating the illusion that you have duplicated my feat.

Let's try a number projection first. Give everyone a pad of paper and a pencil and tell them to write down a three-digit number, with all the digits different, taking care not to show the number to anyone. Now tell them to reverse the order of the digits, creating another three-digit number. Instruct them to subtract the smaller of the two numbers from the larger. For example, 471 reversed yields 174, which is then to be subtracted from 471, yielding in this example 297 (471−174=297). The digits of the total are to be similarly reversed and then added to the original total. In our example, 297 plus 792 yields 1,089. When audience members have arrived at a total, ask those having a four-digit number to raise their hands. All those who do will also have arrived at 1,089, apparently demonstrating your ability at mass projection, while in fact demonstrating the consistency of mathematics![1]

A BONUS "THOUGHT PROJECTION" TEST

Here is a similar test, but one that is best if performed for a single individual. Let me use you as my subject and assume that your first name is spelled with six letters, and that I know this in advance (by the way, how did I know that?). Follow the directions and watch what happens. First, write down the year of your birth. Under this, write down the year that some important event in your life took place, perhaps a graduation, marriage or the birth of a child. You now have two four-digit numbers (unless you are the proverbial thousand-year-old man), one under the other. Under these, write down the number of letters in your first name. Use six in this example. Under that, write

[1]Incidentally, anyone who carried out your instructions but did not arrive at a four-digit result will instead have arrived at a three-digit total, 189. This will only happen for those who start with a number in which the first and last digits differ by one, such as 473. (473 − 374 = 99. 99 + 99 = 189.) Statistically, this will happen less than one-third of the time (two-ninths of the time, to be precise), but when it does, you can still give them credit for sensing three of the four digits you were projecting, missing only the zero. And after all, it's very hard for an intelligent audience to concentrate on nothing!

your age, and finally, under everything, write down the number of years since the aforementioned important event took place. Now add the total of these five numbers. If you are performing this in 1995, the total will be 3,996. This is because the sum of your year of birth and your age will be 1,995, as will the sum of the important event's year and the number of years since it happened: $1,995+1,995=3,990$. Added to this is the problem's only variable, the number of letters in the subject's first name. Obviously, any interesting number that you know in advance can be used for the variable portion; for example, the number of people in the room, the day of the month or the local zip code. Add this to 3,990 to come up with the number that you will attempt to "project" to your subject. Unfortunately, given the high degree of numerical ineptitude in today's society, I predict you will have a few failures unless you remember to bring a calculator for your subject to use!

A KRESKIN COMPULSION EXPERIMENT

On page 100 is a diagram resembling a checkerboard. It consists of sixteen "windows," eight are circles and eight are squares. Inside each window is the name of a celebrity. You may wish to make a larger version of this pattern for your demonstrations, perhaps even drawing it on a chalkboard, and you may substitute your name for mine and those of your friends for those of the other celebrities. When you are ready to begin, point out to the participants that they will be able to move in straight lines, either up and down vertically, side to side horizontally, or diagonally. Of course, they cannot move outside the borders of the board. You should memorize the following instructions so you'll be able to give them with your back to the board. That should be easy, as there are only five moves. In fact, try them now so you'll experience the effect.

First, place your finger on any name that is in a square. You can look for a favorite, or choose one at random. Now move your finger left or right to the nearest circle. Next move up or down to the nearest square. Now move diagonally to the nearest circle. Finally, move either right or down to the nearest square. Incredibly, you will have arrived at the one square bearing the name "Kreskin"!

If you do this for a group, with each participant following along on his or her own board, the effect is positively eerie. On my television series, which was syndicated worldwide, I performed this for Bill Shatner of *Star Trek* fame as a demonstration of how paranormal phenomena could be faked. He found it most intriguing, but I have often wondered how his television counterpart Mr. Spock would have reacted! "Eminently logical," would probably have been his response, because the structure actually demands that anyone who follows my directions will end up on the Kreskin square.

In my performances I often use mental means to influence the thinking and responses of individuals, groups and even the entire audience. These examples will allow you to create the illusion that you can do so, too.

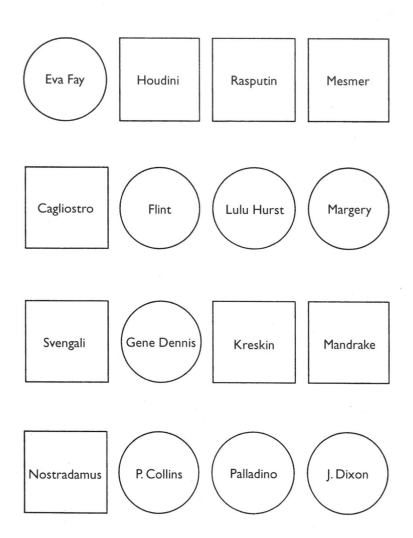

YOU WILL FIND YOURSELF
DRAWN TO "KRESKIN"

CAUGHT "RED-HANDED"

We've all played the guessing game in which a friend hides an object, such as a coin or a piece of candy, in one hand, both being out of sight either behind the back or under the table, and we then try to guess which hand it's in once both are brought into view. On the face of it, there is a fifty-fifty chance of our guess being right, but I will show you a slight variation on this theme that will allow you to achieve a one hundred percent success rate!

Start playing the game with your friends by placing an object in one of your hands behind your back, bringing both hands forward closed into fists and letting your friends guess which hand it is in. Some will be right and some will be wrong. If doing this for just one friend, repeat it three or four times, making sure some failures are included. It should be obvious to all that only guessing is involved. Now for the test.

Let's assume you are doing this for three, four or five people simultaneously, which makes for a more intriguing presentation. Turn your back to the subjects, telling them to pick whatever small object they want, place it in one of their hands, and then hold that hand against their forehead, concentrating on that hand and the fact that it holds the object. Tell them to keep concentrating on that thought, perhaps even for twenty or thirty seconds, to fix it firmly in mind. You explain that in a moment you are going to turn around, so in anticipation of this, they should hold both fists palm down in front of themselves and with the hands level, about waist-high. You turn around and immediately go to each subject, grabbing one hand of each and turning it palm up as you say, "This hand holds the object." Incredibly, you will be correct with every person. You can see how this stunt is more effective done with a group simultaneously, than doing it repeatedly with a single subject.

Once again, the secret is ingenious, combining a knowledge of physiology with careful perception. Remember how you instructed your subjects to hold their hands to their foreheads for twenty or thirty seconds, ostensibly to concentrate on the hands? In fact, the real reason was to allow the blood in the hands time to drain somewhat, thanks to gravity. The result is that when both hands are held side by side, the hand that had been raised to the forehead will be slightly, but perceptibly, lighter than its counterpart. By the time they have turned over their hands and opened them up, the blood will have reached equal levels, destroying the evidence!

COLOR DIVINATION

Occasionally over the years, rather than have subjects think of a name, a series of digits or even a picture, I have asked them to paint a color in their minds or picture a scene in which a single color predominates. This is an interesting exercise and a departure from the more traditional thought-reading experiments.

Here I am going to show you how to create the illusion

that you can perceive a color being thought of by your subject. You'll need a small, opaque paper bag and a box of crayons, the more colors in the box the better. Hold both the open crayon box and the open paper bag behind your back, one in each hand. Ask your subject to take the crayon box, select and remove one crayon from it, hand you the crayon and then close up the box, all of this done behind your back. When you are handed the crayon, you immediately drop it into the bag, which you then crumple up and hand to your subject for safekeeping. The assisting spectator now holds both the closed crayon box and the crumpled bag containing the chosen crayon. Point out that both are closed and opaque, offering no clue as to the contents. Ask the spectator to hold the paper bag up to the light, pointing out that no one can see the contents. Ask the spectator to shake the bag, pointing out that this also gives no clue as to the color of the crayon. Now place both your hands around the bag and crush it further, as though you were sensing the color through the bag. You now announce a color, stating, for example, that the crayon is purple. Your subject will admit with surprise that this is the chosen color, and you then dramatically rip open the bag to extract the crayon, which you display triumphantly.

Of course, there is no real telepathy involved in this stunt, which merely imitates one of my demonstrations. The secret is well hidden as it takes place behind your back. When the spectator assisting you hands you the crayon, you ask him or her to close the crayon box. While the spectator is briefly occupied with this, drop the cho-

sen crayon into the bag, but in the process nick one of the ends of the crayon with a thumbnail, leaving a bit of its color under your nail. You immediately close the bag and hand it to the spectator. When you later place your hands around the bag to crush it further, a quick glance at your thumbnail will tell you all you need to know.

Another, very different, presentation of this stunt would be to claim to your audience that you can always tell when someone is lying. To prove it, have a crayon placed in the bag, as before, but this time, instead of crushing the bag, tell the spectator to answer No to each of your questions. Then ask, "Is the crayon red? Is the crayon black?" and so on. When the spectator says No to the color under your fingernail, tell everyone it's a lie and rip open the bag to prove it.

A SPECIAL KRESKIN BOOK TEST

Over the years I have featured the following test many times in televised and personal appearances: Upon arriving in a city, I will be seen strolling down the street, entering a bookstore or a library and inviting someone to choose any one of the thousands of books, turn to any one of its pages and then concentrate on any one of its words, phrases or diagrams, which I then attempt to divine. The second time Bill Shatner was a guest on my series, he was invited to participate in such a test. But when he arrived in Ottowa, Canada, for the broadcast it was just after six in the evening and the bookstore he went to had already closed for the day. Fortunately, the owner recognized the famous face of the gentleman tapping on his store window and immediately opened the door. He allowed Mr. Shatner to purchase three books, which were then wrapped and sealed and brought to the studio in that condition. On the air, Bill Shatner unsealed the package, chose one of the books, turned to a page and concentrated on a phrase. I received the visual impression of someone being stabbed in the back. As it turned out, the book he had chosen was a murder mystery and the sentence he had chosen described just such a scene!

Now let me show you how to fake such a test without telepathic skills.

Take a fair-size book, one with at least one hundred pages, but preferably with two or three hundred, if not more. Stick the joker from a deck of cards into the book like a bookmark, protruding about an inch. Take a look at and remember what is on the page it marks. If the page has a picture, so much the better. Approach your subject with the book in hand, holding it with the protruding card away from the spectator and covered by the hand holding the book. With your other hand, give the spectator a deck of cards and instruct him or her to remove the joker from the deck (either use a deck having two identical jokers, or buy a matching deck to obtain the second joker) and insert it into the end of the book. Make sure that the joker being inserted faces the same way (faceup or facedown) as the duplicate joker at the other end. When the joker has been inserted partway, ask the spectator to come forward and follow you to a table. As you turn away from the audience to go to the table, quickly push the spectator's joker all the way into the book and turn the book end for end to bring your protruding joker to the book's outer end. When you turn to face the audience again, they will see a joker protruding from the end of the book, just as before, except that this is your joker, marking your page. Hand the book to the spectator with the request that he or she rest the book on the ta-

ble and open it to the page marked by the card. It is important to have the book on the table, rather than in the spectator's hands, to prevent the other joker from falling out of the book. Stand with your back to the audience as the spectator opens to the page and begins to concentrate on its contents. After a pause to heighten the drama and give the spectator time to read most of the page, begin to describe what is being read. Since it is the page you chose in advance, you should be able to do so with one hundred percent accuracy, even without telepathic abilities!

TELEPORTATION

The following stunt was a favorite of the great Houdini. We are told that he liked to do this for private gatherings at his home, at banquets, and even at meetings of the Society of American Magicians, over which he presided for many years prior to his death in 1926. You'll be able to do this with people standing all around you, carefully watching every move. Take out an old coin or some other intriguing small object about which you can weave an interesting story, such as a rusty key from a haunted house, a good luck talisman from an Indian Yogi or a Gypsy's finger ring. Introduce the object and openly place it on the palm of your left hand. Take an opaque handkerchief with your right hand and carefully cover the left hand, pointing out that you will not touch the hand as you cover it. This, you explain, is because everyone knows that there are swift and secret means of stealing such an object by sleight of hand and you want everyone to be absolutely certain at this point that it is still on the left palm, even though they can't see it.

Often someone will express doubt concerning the object's whereabouts at this point, which is perfect for your purposes. Ask that person to reach under the handkerchief and verify by touch that the object is still there. Should no one express such doubts, simply ask someone to reach under the handkerchief to feel the object. They will testify that the object is still on the left palm. Ask another person to repeat this action, then another, and another until there truly can be no doubt regarding the existence and location of the object. At that point, draw attention to your right hand by snapping its fingers over the handkerchief. Announce that the coin has been mysteriously teleported and then grab one corner of the handkerchief with the right hand and instantly pull it off the left hand. The coin has vanished without a trace. Magicians are often accused of using their sleeves to accomplish their tricks, but this can be done with the sleeves rolled up. In fact, you could feature this at a nudist colony! Later, as people mill around, someone will suddenly spot the ring on the side of a chair or on a shelf, having apparently been paranormally teleported to that location.

This mysterious feat is accomplished through the subtle use of a secret assistant. You need only make sure that your accomplice is the last person to feel the object under the handkerchief. Not only does he or she feel it, but actually steals it away in a loosely closed hand while verbally confirming its presence on your palm! You then place some distance between yourself and your accomplice as you talk about the mysterious event about to transpire. This gives your assistant a chance to set the object down casually where it will be discovered later. Once you whisk away the handkerchief, everyone will begin looking around to see where it might have gone. You'll be surprised by their reaction when they spontaneously find it, another example of the powerful force of the human imagination, focused in this case on the theme of teleportation.

THEM BONES, THEM BONES...

In my television appearances, I often use dice to introduce an element of chance and spontaneity when choosing numbers. After all, fair dice cannot be controlled unless one has the rare gift that pioneer parapsychologist Dr. J. B. Rhine termed "psychokinesis" nearly fifty years

ago. Here's a fun way to simulate such an ability. You will apparently take two dice and drop them in an oversize matchbox (with the wooden matches removed, of course). A member of your audience shakes the dice in the box and you then call out two numbers. When you slowly open the box, those two numbers are seen to be uppermost on the dice. Did you clairvoyantly penetrate the cardboard matchbox, or was it a demonstration of psychokinesis?

Actually, it demonstrates the value of advance preparation when staging such a pseudodemonstration! Beforehand you glued two dice to the bottom of the inside at one end of the matchbox drawer. Place the two matching loose dice in the drawer at the other end and you are all set. When ready to perform, push out the end of the matchbox drawer with the loose dice and dump them out onto the table. Since the other two dice are neither seen (being hidden by the sleeve of the match-box) nor heard, their presence will never be suspected. Throw the loose dice on the table several times to demonstrate their fairness, then drop them in the matchbox and hand it out to be shaken.

When you take the box back, shake it just enough to make sure the loose dice settle at the end away from the fixed dice. Call out the numbers and push open the drawer to reveal the fixed dice with the predicted numbers uppermost.

A MOMENT OF REFLECTION

In this stunt you will be able to reveal two-digit numbers that audience members have written on blank cards and placed in a goblet facing away from you. One at a time, you'll reach into the goblet and remove a card, writing side facing away from you, yet be able to reveal the freely chosen number while holding the card against your forehead. This imitates my feat of telling people their phone numbers, social security numbers and other private information, but you won't need telepathic abilities!

What you do need is a cuff link with a shiny, mirrorlike surface, such as can be found in the men's section of any decent department store. Close the cuff link, to shorten its stem, which you clip at the fleshy base of your first and second fingers, with the cuff link inside the hand. Held properly, no one looking at the back of your hand will suspect the presence of a mirrored cuff link inside your hand. As you hold the goblet aloft with one hand, the other hand, concealing the mirrored cuff link, moves to the front of the glass to remove a card, affording you ample opportunity to see the reflection of that card's numbers in the cuff link's mirrored surface. So you literally are "reflecting" the audience's thoughts, not to mention the cards themselves.

MAGNETIC PERSONALITIES

The fall of the old Soviet Empire has coincided with a resurgence of activity by self-styled Russian psychics, producing at least one apparently new phenomenon. It is claimed that an energy emanating from some psychics attracts metals as though their bodies had magnetic properties.

There is no question that we can control some of the energies our bodies produce. Backstage visitors after my performances frequently comment on the intense heat pouring from my hands, often sensing it from more than a foot and a half away. The concentrated energy that I must harness to succeed in my demonstrations is somehow reflected in the heat from my hands, which grows in intensity with my programs. This admission does not mean that I accept the Russian psychics' claims to be able to magnetize their bodies. As one proof of their claims, photographs have been published showing coins clinging to the psychics' foreheads. But when I was a kid, I learned a simple trick that seems to have been forgotten today and exactly simulates this "new phenomenon."

Borrow a coin and have it examined so everyone can make sure there is nothing sticky on it. As this is being done, talk about the Russian psychics' "discovery" and related mysterious energy outpourings, such as the heat from my hands we just mentioned. Take back the coin and press it flat against your forehead. If your skin is moist, the coin will cling easily, but if your skin is somewhat dry, press the coin flat and then push it upward an eighth of an inch or so before slowly releasing your hand. The coin will stay in position. You can even take another coin and press it on the other side of your forehead to compound the image of metal mysteriously clinging to your body.

GET THE LEAD OUT

You can follow up the coin stunt by telling your friends that you have found a way to control your energy fields to attract even nonmetallic objects. Take a pencil out of your pocket and let people touch it to confirm there is nothing sticky on it. Then hold the fingers of one hand together and press the pencil against them, causing it to cling to them. You can turn your hand upside down, sideways, and even swing it through the air with the pencil staying in position. After a few moments of this you can reach over with the other hand and remove the pencil, allowing people to feel your fingers to make sure they are not sticky either.

In fact, neither the fingers nor the pencil is sticky, but you do need to prepare the pencil in advance. Break a pin so that it is only about one-quarter-inch long, then hammer it into the pencil, leaving just enough sticking out for you to clip between two fingers when the pencil is placed against them. If the pencil is placed near your fingertips, you can get a very firm grip on the pin and the pencil will seem to cling magnetically no matter how you

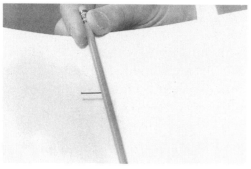

move your hand. The small projection from the pin allows you to hide it from view simply by curling a finger around as you display the pencil. Since you allow them to feel the pencil's surface before the demonstration, they will want to examine your hand afterward, giving you plenty of time to pocket the pencil.

8

JUST CHECKING...

For most of my career, my signature test as a mentalist has been the risking of my performance fee at a climactic point in my program. Here is an actual description of what I have been doing for many years now: First, my check is turned over to a committee of strangers from the audience. I am then escorted from the theater, auditorium or banquet hall by a second committee of audience members who establish that I cannot see or hear what is taking place inside the auditorium. During my absence, the committee with the check proceeds to hide it anywhere inside the auditorium or arena. Once this is done, I am brought back to the stage by the second committee, whose members verify that I had no opportunity to see or hear what happened in my absence. I then have at least one member of the first committee concentrate on the location of the check, which I proceed to find, directed only by his or her thoughts.

No questions are asked, no comments are made, and should I fail mentally to pick up sufficient ideas for me to pinpoint the actual location of the check, then it is my agreed commitment to return the check to the corporation, organization or theater sponsoring my program and forfeit my fee. Even after many years of performing this feat on a regular basis, I am still amazed at the ingenuity of my audiences. At the University of Alabama I actually found the bill inside the barrel of a security guard's revolver and at Northwestern it was above the upper plate of a gentleman's false teeth—which he was wearing at the time! And I don't think I'll ever forget my appearance at a Bob Hope dinner at the Waldorf-Astoria when I found the check cooked inside the stuffing of a turkey on the dais!

Recently I passed through the audience of the university theater in which I was presenting one of my concerts and entered the lobby, where I encountered some students playing catch. I had an irresistible urge to reach into one of the ballplayer's shirt pockets and though I didn't find the check there, I did find a penknife, which gave me a clue. Within a matter of moments I had used the knife to peel back the skin of the ball to find my check stitched inside it!

Even more vivid in my mind are the near failures, which still haunt my memory. One of the most dramatic took place recently in Owensboro, Kentucky. I was performing my second show of the day, and was gratified that my audience of country music fans was sharing the same enthusiasm for my work as have other audiences all over the world.

The first show had gone without a hitch. The committee responsible for hiding the check during my second show signaled my escorts that the time had come for me to return to the nightclub auditorium to find the check. After briefly roaming through the audience, I quickly made my way to the back of the club where I found a series of wooden surfaces, like desktops, with dishes, knives, forks, napkins and other sundry items stacked on top of them. I opened the door to one of the containers, but it was black inside and seemed to lead no further. I picked another committee member to guide my thoughts mentally and tried again. Once again, after a brief roam through the audience, I returned to the container at the back, but again when I reached inside it, I drew a blank and couldn't sense how to proceed. After several minutes of frustration, perhaps as many as three (though it seemed an eternity to me at the time), I asked for yet another committee member and tried again, but with identical results.

Twenty-five of the most frustrating minutes of my career later, I became confused and decided to give up. Whenever this has happened in the past, inevitably someone in the audience believes this is purely show-manship on my part, a ploy to heighten interest in the test by dramatizing the conflict. But, in fact, though each of the committee members with whom I'd worked had mentally guided me to the same location, none had been able to provide any further guidance. I turned to the audience and announced that this appeared to be my tenth and final failure, as I had resolved to retire the test from my performances should I fail a tenth time. But some-thing inside me told me that things were not quite what they should have been and I began to get annoyed. Nothing about this test seemed right and I decided to give it another try with yet another committee member. Once again I was compelled to return to the same location at the back of the nightclub, but once there, drew a complete blank. Now I was both frustrated and angry! If you read an account of this incident in the next day's newspaper, you would have read a slight distortion of what actually took place. The article implied that I had reneged on the conditions of the test, since I did not give back the money and had apparently suffered a legitimate failure. That was not the case. Something prompted me to ask a particular member of the committee to retrieve the check. Ironically, she went to the exact location where I had been drawing a blank, opened the door and reached inside at about waist height. After her hand groped around inside for a few moments, it emerged empty. I asked another committee member to retrieve the check, and the same scenario was repeated. Then it dawned on me. My primary condition has always been that each committee member must know *exactly* where the check is hidden. In this case, only one of them did, the one who had hidden it! The others, watching from a slight distance, really had no idea of the "exact" location of the check. I was put in a position I have always feared: Trying to perceive the thoughts of someone not fully aware of the true state of affairs.

Thank goodness I caught this, for the committee had inadvertently and quite innocently not complied with my conditions. I immediately rounded up another committee, had the same check hidden, and after returning to the auditorium found myself moving my fingers along a darkened area of the back wall in less than one minute. I sensed a splinter in the wall and pulled on it. Incredibly, the check had been fed into this splinterlike seam!

Once again I was reminded that without the concentration of my audience, be it a single individual or several thousand, it would be impossible for me to succeed with any of my thought-reading tests. My nine failures to date continue to haunt me, including the time at a large arena in New Zealand when I forfeited my fee of nearly fifty-one thousand dollars! It was donated to a hospital for crippled children and I take some consolation in having been told that they have named a new wing after me. But, to be truthful, I felt at the time as though I might need temporary psychological hospitalization myself!

In the past few decades no one has duplicated this test on a regular basis. Some have faked it by having the check placed inside a wallet, which is then hidden. Of course, a wallet is not only much more difficult to hide effectively, but in this case it was actually electronically wired to generate a signal that the so-called mind reader could sense as he got closer to it! Others have used paid assistants in the audience—"stooges"—who would give instructions to the "psychic" using sophisticated "walkie-talkies," the receiving device being hidden under a turban worn by the performer.

One episode of the TV series "Friday the Thirteenth" centered on a fraudulent television mentalist who featured the check finding feat, using a secret hearing aid to gain the information he needed. I was contacted by the writers of the show, who wanted to pattern their staging on my legitimate demonstrations, even though the character in their horror story was using trickery. Now I have never used and will never use confederates or stooges or electronic devices in my work. In fact, I have a standing offer of fifty thousand dollars payable to anyone who can prove that I employ paid assistants or confederates in any aspect of my programs. The television writers contacting me knew this, of course, but wanted to heighten audience interest by making the fictitious staging as realistic as possible. Ultimately, their fake Kreskin got what he deserved, as his hearing aid turned out to be demonically possessed and destroyed him!

Keeping that in mind, here is how you can fake being a Kreskin with a modified version of my legitimate test.

CHECK THIS OUT

Explain how my check is hidden at each of my performances and that I proceed to locate it by thought perception. Explain that you will attempt a Kreskin-like test. When you leave the room, you explain, a committee is to single out one person in the entire room. When you return to the room, everyone is to sit or stand still, without speaking.

You then leave the room, escorted by one or two others who verify that you do not eavesdrop on the room in your absence. When you return, begin to walk quietly around the room. This may be a gathering of ten or fifteen friends, a classroom of thirty or forty, or perhaps even a congregation at a festival with seventy or more present. As you quietly walk through the gathering, suddenly place your hands on someone's shoulder and announce that this is the chosen one. You will be right.

Here is the secret for faking this stunt: You do have a confederate in the audience, a secret assistant, but he does not have any fancy electronic devices to communicate with you. When you ask your audience to become totally silent so that you can concentrate, everyone will turn to watch your progress. As you pass near the chosen person, your secret assistant simply sniffles once or twice. Because of the silence, and because you are listening for it, you will have no trouble picking up this signal. As you focus your attention on specific individuals in that area, your assistant again sniffles discreetly as you approach the chosen person. A sniffle is an entirely natural part of the background noise and will pass completely unnoticed by those not listening for it, though it will be obvious to you.

While you may not have met the Kreskin challenge by using thought transference or telepathy, you can take some pride in the fact that with just a few sniffles you have duplicated what other fake Kreskins needed thousands of dollars of electronics to achieve!

CHECK IN A HAYSTACK

Here is another way to put your check "at risk" while demonstrating the difficulty of the check-finding feat.

Gather together ten or fifteen small envelopes, about the size of pay envelopes, and two clear plastic bags.

Crush one of the bags so that it is very wrinkled, then place the other bag upside down inside the crushed bag. The wrinkles in the outer bag make it impossible to detect that what you really have is a transparent purse with two compartments, the upside down inner bag serving as a wall to separate the two sides. On one side place the many envelopes that have only a blank piece of paper sealed inside. On the other side place a single envelope in which you have sealed your check, or if you prefer, a twenty-dollar bill. If you now shake the bag, taking care to hold the inner bag in place to keep the compartments intact, the envelopes will spread in disarray, making it impossible to discern the fact that there is a lone envelope on one side of the bag, particularly if you take care to hold that side away from the audience.

Having apparently mixed the envelopes, open the bag to the compartment with the many envelopes, holding the inner bag against the side with the single envelope containing your money. Invite five, six, seven or even eight people to remove envelopes from the bag, telling them that they will be unable to find the one envelope containing the money. This can be dramatized by offering to burn their envelopes and also by giving them a chance to exchange envelopes before they open them. Once the spectators have their envelopes and only five or six remain in the bag, grasp the bag by its bottom edge and dump the remaining envelopes onto the table. The lone envelope will fall out with the others and blend in with them on the table.

Once the spectators have opened their envelopes and

discovered only a blank piece of paper, open the remaining five or six envelopes to show that one of them did indeed contain your check or money, which you somehow were able to prevent them from finding.

9
THE KRESKIN READINGS

Without any doubt, the greatest response to my television work has been generated by my successful attempts to tune in to the spontaneous thoughts of my studio audiences. This was pointed out many years ago by Roger Ailes, then producer of "The Mike Douglas Show," and has been confirmed time and again by the volume of viewer mail and phone calls that these demonstrations invariably elicit. Roger felt such a demonstration should always be an integral part of my appearances with Mike, time permitting, since it established my ability to scan an audience mentally and helped the home viewers realize that were they in the studio, the same thing would be happening to them.

I've shown you many practical methods for imitating and faking my demonstrations. Some of the theories proposed by others to "explain" my work should really be classified as science fiction, they are so fantastic and outrageous. In fact, recently some rather "enterprising" individuals offered to sell the supposed "secrets" of my performances for hundreds of dollars, and even had the audacity to use my name in their ads! Since they felt no compunction about invoking my name, I feel that I am within my rights to save you the money by revealing here the "secrets" they were selling. They claim that while I am passing out envelopes, slips of paper used by audience members for jotting down questions and thoughts are secretly stolen by sleight of hand or switched for bogus slips of paper that are placed in the envelopes. Thus the envelopes, which are kept by the audience, supposedly no longer contain the secret thoughts they were intended to safeguard. Sometime later, it is claimed, I use sleight of hand (again!) to hide the stolen slips behind a large writing tablet. The tablet is supposedly covered with glue so that I can stick the slips (which I secretly unfold) all over it! If you have as much imagination as the authors of this high-priced exposé, then it won't take much of a stretch for you to picture me pretending to write on the glue- and slip-covered pad, while actually (they claim) reading the many open slips.

Of course, there is still some potentially incriminating evidence that must be dealt with in this not-ready-for-prime-time scenario: the sealed envelopes in the audience. According to them, I find an excuse to take the purloined envelopes from the audience and throw them in an attaché case "for safekeeping," as though audience members cannot be trusted with their own thoughts! In all fairness to the mystery merchants attempting to sell these "secrets," you did get more than a mere manuscript for your money. Purchasers received a strange pad made of cheap cardboard with side barriers to hide the "dirty work." You don't need to be Kreskin to predict in advance that their offer does not come with a money-back guarantee!

THE TELEPATHY ILLUSION

It would be impossible for me to teach you here the techniques that I began to develop as an adolescent and that now enable me to tune in to the thoughts of perfect strangers. But I can show you a more practical and realistic way of simulating my readings than the overpriced pipe dream discussed above. This will enable you to create a convincing illusion that you are "doing a Kreskin."

Begin by passing out slips of paper to your guests. There could be thirty or more, or as few as six or seven. Invite your friends to jot down a question, perhaps about an upcoming event or future decision they are contemplating. Incidentally, this stunt has long been used by fraudulent spirit mediums to gain access to the questions that séance clients would like directed to their departed loved ones. Please, do not present it in this manner. Not only is it in questionable taste, but to take advantage of people who may be seriously bereaved is patently unconscionable.

Ask that the papers be folded with the questions on the inside so that no one else can see what they've written, then have the slips collected. You need not collect them yourself; in fact, it will be more impressive if you do not. The collected slips should be in a hat or bag or similar receptacle large enough to hold them. Reach into the container and remove one of the slips, holding the folded slip against your forehead. Concentrate for a moment and then say, "Somebody is considering buying or investing in telephone stocks, but doubts that this is the right time to do it. Who wrote that question?" When the individual identifies him- or herself, unfold the paper, read it to yourself, and then discard the slip by placing it in your pocket. Proceed to give a very general response to the question, without urging any particular decision. You might say that the answer will come to the questioner quite clearly after some private reflection, but that he or she should be careful not to be swayed too much by the advice of others, who may wish to encourage their own agenda.

Now remove another slip of paper from the receptacle, apparently read the writer's mind, and when he or she stands to acknowledge the question, you again offer a brief comment. This process may be continued indefinitely, but my advice is to keep it short. After four or five such readings, it takes a clever showman indeed to sustain interest beyond the individual whose specific question is being addressed.

Here is how you are able to accomplish this feat: One person in the audience is in league with you. You have agreed beforehand that he or she will write a specific, known question on his or her slip and then fold it in a distinctly recognizable fashion, so that it will be obvious to you but not the casual observer. In our example, the assistant wrote the question about the telephone stock. When the slips are all collected, you are ready to begin.

Reach inside the container and remove any slip except the one written by your secret assistant, and hold it to your forehead. Announce the question written by your accomplice, who stands to acknowledge it, acting a little surprised at your success. You open the slip, apparently to confirm the question, but really to read and memorize the question that is actually on the paper, which will be dealt with next. The audience, of course, assumes that you are looking at the question written by your secret accomplice. Having read and memorized the question, place it in your pocket, removing the incriminating evidence from the audience arena.

After the generalized response to your accomplice's question, pick out a second slip from the receptacle (again taking care that it is not the accomplice's slip), concentrate for a moment with the folded slip against your forehead, and then announce the question you just read on the first slip, requesting the questioner to stand. Once again, open the slip to read the next question, as you proceed to answer the second question in general terms.

When you are ready to conclude the experiment, take your accomplice's slip out of the receptacle and respond to the question you just read on the previous slip, placing the final slip in your pocket after "reading" it. This leaves you "clean," in that the slips in your pocket really do correspond to the questions you addressed.

Although this stunt merely simulates a portion of my own program, don't underestimate its potential. It has been the "stock-in-trade" of fraudulent spirit mediums for at least 150 years and continues to be used to convince congregations in many spiritualistic communities. In picking an accomplice, choose someone who will not "blow the gaff" and reveal your secret, thus destroying the mystery that you have created. Also take care to keep your answers very general as those who sincerely seek advice from "psychics" often place such confidence in the responses as to make them self-fulfilling predictions. You should not assume the role of a cult leader and take responsibility for the life decisions of others in the guise of a false prophet. You should, instead, simply be entertaining your friends with a few well-chosen and rehearsed Kreskin-like feats.

CONCLUSION

In the previous pages I have shared with you the theories that others have proposed to explain away the legitimate phenomena that I present in my performances. At the very same time, I have shared with you numerous angles and subterfuges to allow you to imitate some of what I do for the amusement of your friends. In so doing, it has never been my intention to discredit legitimate phenomena, whether exhibited by myself or others, but simply to give you an opportunity to share in the joy and excitement of the performance of these feats.

Never think of me as a debunker. For even as I expose hypnosis to be a purely imaginary phenomenon, I always point out the tremendous and very real power of pure imagination itself. It is both tragic and deplorable that so many self-styled skeptics are, in fact, merely cynics.

As you go through life, never stop asking questions, but always keep in mind that information can never be a substitute for imagination. Indeed, information by itself is worthless until transformed into ideas through the power of creative imagination. If you use your imagination with wisdom, compassion and optimism, I can assure you that the reward will be a lifetime of joyous adven-

ture. Be the good Lord willin', our paths will cross again soon on that adventure and until they do, you have my very best thoughts . . .

—KRESKIN